# The Cornwall gardens guide

by
## Douglas Ellory Pett

With a Foreword by
## Sir Richard Carew Pole
President of the Cornwall Gardens Trust

Alison Hodge

First published in 2003 by
Alison Hodge
Bosulval, Newmill, Penzance, Cornwall TR20 8XA
info@alison-hodge.co.uk  www.alison-hodge.co.uk

ISBN 0 906720 32 X

British Library Cataloguing-in-Publication Data
A catalogue record for this book is available from the
British Library.

Designed by Christopher Laughton
Originated by BDP – Book Development & Production,
Penzance, Cornwall
Printed in Spain

# Contents

# Foreword by Sir Richard Carew Pole, President of the Cornwall Gardens Trust

Nothing gives me more pleasure than to write the Foreword for this splendid Guidebook. Cornish garden-owners have made a tremendous contribution to the history of gardening in this country. Throughout the 19th and 20th centuries, gardens have been developed in Cornwall by imaginative and creative owners, some of whom have been plant-hunters, or have supported others in their search for unusual plants in some of the world's remotest parts. This generation can now benefit from seeing mature plants and trees collected by these early expeditions growing and flourishing in our unique climate.

Cornwall is well known for its wide diversity of gardens, and Douglas Pett must be congratulated on putting together this book, which will provide guidance and inspiration for all garden-lovers wherever they may come from.

Richard Carew Pole
Antony House, Torpoint

The Cornwall Gardens Guide is the most comprehensive guide to the gardens of Cornwall, and perhaps of any county in England. It includes over 120 gardens, public and country parks that open regularly, and a supplementary list of significant historic gardens that are accessible only occasionally.

For each garden there are map references, road directions, and full details for enquiries. Typical opening times and facilities are listed, and the pronunciation of Cornish place-names – often puzzling to visitors – is explained. English Heritage gradings in their Register of buildings and artifacts, and in the Register of gardens, as well as national and local designations for landscape beauty are included, to indicate those places officially recognized – although this in no way suggests that many other gardens are not equally, and in some cases more worth visiting.

Practical gardeners will welcome the notes for each of the main gardens on size, altitude, aspect, average rainfall and temperature, and soil – each of which affects the growth of plants.

The Guide is lavishly illustrated with photographs of the location and special features of the gardens, and specimens of individual flowers, many of which are characteristic of the local climate, and some (like those on Tresco, to the right) rarely seen in the open elsewhere. The Introduction looks at the geology and climate of the region, and at the development of horticulture and design through the ages, especially in relation to Cornish gardens.

Further information about the wealth of historic gardens in Cornwall may be found in the definitive The Parks and Gardens of Cornwall[1], which is illustrated with historic prints and contains detailed references. Plant-lovers are referred to W. Arnold-Forster's classic Shrubs for the Milder Counties[2], and the forthcoming Gardening on the Edge[3], which describes present-day experiences.

Douglas Ellory Pett
March 2003

1 Pett, D.E., 1998, The Parks and Gardens of Cornwall, Alison Hodge.
2 Arnold-Forster, W., 2000, Shrubs for the Milder Counties, 2nd edn, Alison Hodge.
3 Gardening on the Edge, Alison Hodge (forthcoming).

# Preface

The first impression of a visitor to Cornwall is that it is quite un-English. Crossing the bridge over the Tamar at once induces a sense of isolation. Here are no large towns, such as Plymouth or Exeter. Villages are scattered, clustering around crossroads, or along a highway, often with the church standing apart. The windswept plateaux, out of which rise great granite bosses, are covered with a tapestry of small, squarish fields, surrounded by stone- or slate-walled hedges, dotted at surprisingly regular intervals with isolated farmsteads. Everywhere are the relics of antiquity, and the wastes of mining and quarrying.

# Introduction

Out of this historic landscape sprang up the manor houses and mansions, set in luxuriant gardens and parks, which were influenced by, and utilized the unique features of the terrain. Before looking at the history of these estates, we shall examine briefly the physical characteristics that moulded their shape.

## Geology and soil

Cornwall forms the western projection of 'Highland Britain'. The peninsula runs in a south-west – north-east direction, narrowing from about 50 miles (80km) at its widest point in the east, to an average of 20 miles (32km), with most of the region within five to eight miles (8–13km) of the coast or a tidal estuary, thus everywhere experiencing a more or less maritime climate.

The underlying formations are of two kinds – granite, or 'killas' (the country rock). The soil over the granite is typically peaty and acid, so by choice very few of the gardens are found there. Where the granite thrusts through the killas, the rock became heated and created changed – 'metamorphic' – forms, and it was in these regions that minerals were deposited that brought wealth to the great mining areas of St Just, Camborne–Redruth and Callington.

Around St Austell the granite decayed into china clay, which was of equal economic importance, leading to the growth of a prosperous town where, during the 18th and 19th centuries, many new gardens were created.

However, not all of the killas was fertile. Along the north coast it produced a sticky clay which, combined with strong winds was not conducive to horticulture, so here mansions are thin on the ground. To the south, the serpentines of the Lizard peninsula formed another area where the soil is unfavorable to cultivation, only **Bonython** (5) and **Trelowarren** (27), which lie off the serpentine, being successful.

The highest quality soils are found in three areas: in the west, a triangle running from Lelant to Perranuthnoe and Penzance, which encompasses the gardens of **Trewidden** (31), **Trengwainton** (28; photo page 7) and **Trevarno** (30); in the east, the slopes of the Tamar Valley, between Callington and Saltash, are the site for **Cotehele** (92), **Pentillie Castle** (118), **Antony** (89) and **Ince Castle** (97); but it is the central area, along the western side of the Fal estuary up to Truro, that the highest density of Cornish gardens are found, among them **Carclew** (35), the three Fox gardens, and the oldest estate of all – **Enys** (114). Even so, it was as much the topography as the soil that led to their success. **Trebah** (51) and **Glendurgan** (38), as well as **Bosahan** (110) and other gardens on the Helford estuary, are all 'ravine' or valley gardens. So it is no surprise that in the valleys of the Fowey and Looe rivers there are similar concentrations; indeed, it is the estuaries that embrace the majority of the more celebrated parks and gardens in Cornwall.

## Climate

For the horticulturist, climate is an inexact science, since every garden has its own frost-pockets and hot-spots. However, there are trends that make the weather in Cornwall unusual, if not unique.

### Rainfall and humidity

Rainfall is on average some ten inches (25.5cm) less than on Dartmoor, Wales and other similar areas, and closely reflects the topography, rising towards the higher moorland, with the driest areas along the north coast. Perhaps of equal importance for the growth of plants is the humidity, which in Cornwall is unusually high, averaging around 80 per cent. This is welcomed by species such as camellias, rhododendrons and conifers, for which Cornwall is celebrated, but causes frustrating damping off in other varieties that originate in drier climes.

### Temperature

The climate of Cornwall is warmer and more equable than anywhere else in Britain, but this is commonly misunderstood by those with little experience of gardening here. The frequent use of the expression 'sub-tropical' conjures up an imaginary land of hot summers and frost-free winters, where bananas and date palms flourish. A glance at a temperature chart will at once dispel any such illusions. 'Equable' signifies a climate that has a narrow range between its high and low average temperatures, which in Cornwall is the narrowest in the country. Frosts are infrequent, but it is never very hot in summer. This has important consequences for vegetation, for although for much of the year the temperature does not fall below that required for growth, it is seldom hot enough to provide the roasting needed by some quite hardy plants to ripen and flower.

However, it is probably the lower end of the scale, and especially the occasional extremes that are of most interest to the Cornish gardener who experiments with plants on the margin of hardiness. Whereas rainfall rises over the higher ground, temperature falls. Exceptionally, temperatures of -8°C may be experienced even in the warmest places, and from -10° to -12°C on the Devon border. These figures are 'means' – mid-points – reduced to mean sea level, which fall lower as the ground rises.

In general terms, the procession of seasons in Cornwall differs from that in other parts of the country: spring arrives early, summer late; autumn is long and winter short. In such a climate, even though relatively frost-free, it is the unexpected early or late frost that causes the greatest havoc.

## Wind

As long ago as the 16th century, Norden described the 'fierce & furious wyndes' that 'sharply assayl the naked hills & dales', and nothing has changed. Although no-one escapes, the exposed areas of the extreme west, the Lizard and the north coast suffer most. So from the earliest days the wise Cornishman has sought the shelter of a valley, or a south-east facing slope, with the protection of a screen of trees.

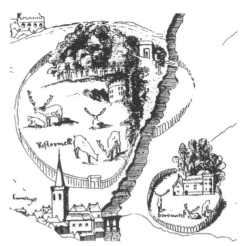

## Garden history

### The beginnings

The remains of the Iron Age 'courtyard houses' at Chysauster, near Penzance, each of which has an enclosure that may have been cultivated, are a good starting point for the history of gardening in Cornwall. They were followed by typical early or 'Celtic' settlements – usually solitary farmsteads, or at most small groups of farms, each with a 'close' attached. In the 12th century, one of the contributions of the Normans was the impaling of nine deer parks, five of which were associated with their castles. Well over 100 deer parks are recorded in Cornwall, which eventually inspired the greater estates to surround their dwellings with parkland. Of these, **Boconnoc** (59; plan above) alone among these ancient parks has survived, the other deer parks being reduced to two only, at **Prideaux Place** (81) and **Tregothnan** (120).

### The medieval period

As times became wilder, many felt the need to provide themselves with protection from marauders. Wealthier residents fortified their dwellings by castellating their houses, building towers, and walling-in their courtyards, perhaps with a gate-house or barbican at the entrance. No complete house of this type survives, but there are enough relics and illustrations to obtain a fair impression of how they might once have appeared. **Cotehele** (92) is the finest example, although it has undergone many alterations. The tower houses at **Boconnoc** (59) and **Godolphin** (10) have been completely replaced, and at **Pengersick** (15) little remains but the tower.

### The 16th century

During the reign of Elizabeth I, the country was more settled and peaceful, and there was no longer any pressing need to fortify houses. As early as 1547, for instance, Sir Richard Edgcumbe's new house at **Mount Edgcumbe** (101), although castellated, was open and outward-looking. Nevertheless a fashion for castles had taken root: the square brick **Ince Castle** (97; photo page 9), a century later, being the first in a long line of pseudo-castles and castellated houses.

Even without fortifications, however, the former pattern of living continued. Typically there would still be a walled forecourt, perhaps with a gatehouse. The various other courtyards fulfilled many functions – a 'green court' where a visitor could 'park' his horse, or a 'herbary' where pot-herbs, salads and green vegetables were grown. There might be fruit, bee or hop gardens too. Remnants of these courtyard gardens have survived here and there, but **Penheale Manor** (103) with inner, front and two side courts is the most intact. Its raised walk, and possible relics of fish ponds add elements essential in the greater houses.

### The 17th and 18th centuries

The Restoration after the Commonwealth marked a watershed in garden design, after which landowners were able to build on a more lavish scale, often with elaborate formal gardens in the Dutch or Italian manner. Such a garden at **Trebartha** (108), quartered, with slender trees at each corner, and statues both in each quarter and in the centre, is illustrated in the manuscript *Spoure Book* of *c*.1690. In the early 18th century, Edmund Prideaux left a finer collection of sketches made during two tours in 1716 and 1727, mostly to houses of his relatives, which show similar elaborate designs at his own **Prideaux Place** (81), **Antony** (89) and other houses. Today, the magnificent Italian and French gardens at **Mount Edgcumbe** (101) alone remain to represent this era.

By the middle of the 18th century, all of these formal gardens were swept aside to make way for the new landscape style. The influence of William Kent, one of the first of these designers, was to be seen at **Werrington** (122), which was adorned with a triumphal arch, temples, a ruined castle, hermitage, and ornamental bridge, set in a landscape of clumped trees. 'Capability' Brown, however, never ventured

as far west as Cornwall, although his ideas were carried back by the aristocracy and gentry who travelled to London, or visited the estates of their fashionable relatives. Moving west, aside from **Mount Edgcumbe** (101), **Port Eliot** (119), **Boconnoc** (59), **Chyverton** (112), **Tehidy** (24) and Clowance (now in time-shares) were all influenced by this new landscape trend.

Towards the end of the 18th century, the political influence of the Pitt family, through their relatives at **Boconnoc** (59) and **Port Eliot** (119), introduced Humphry Repton to Cornwall, where he prepared Red Books for **Antony** (89), **Port Eliot** (119), **Catchfrench** (111) and **Trewarthenick** (121) after his visit in 1792, and for **Tregothnan** (120) and **Pentillie Castle** (118) visited in 1809. But as explained above, the terrain in Cornwall does not lend itself to this style of gardening, and the new century introduced new concepts more suited to the lie of the land.

### The 19th and 20th centuries

Even though Repton continued to be active in the early years of the 19th century, it was John Claudius Loudon who was the more representative of the new century, for he addressed a rising and prosperous middle class. He personally

visited four gardens in Cornwall: **Mount Edgcumbe** (101), **Pentillie Castle** (118), Tor House, and Trematon Castle, and included ten in the gazetteer in his *Encyclopoedia* of 1822, among which **Carclew** (35) perhaps reflected most clearly the new mood among garden-owners. Sir Charles Lemon, who then owned Carclew, was himself a correspondent of the botanists William and his son Joseph Hooker, whom he later sponsored in his Himalayan expedition, and it was on their recommendation that he appointed William Beattie Booth, with botanical skills, as his gardener.

As early as 1811 Worgan, in his survey of agriculture in Cornwall, had remarked on the increased planting of trees, but this was less in the open landscape than in the valleys, at first as windbreaks to protect the new species of trees and shrubs that were increasingly being introduced. Thus the 'valley garden' was to become the most characteristic of all the Cornish innovations. Of these the first, and perhaps the most influential, was **Penjerrick** (45), where it was the skill in the association of the various trees, as well as their range, that impressed contemporary horticultural writers. Robert Were Fox's example was followed by his brothers at **Glendurgan** (38) and **Trebah**

(51; photo left), and emulated at **Heligan** (71) and many other gardens.

The thirst for new varieties continued throughout the 19th century. The brothers William and Thomas Lobb, whose father had worked at **Pencarrow** (77) and later at **Carclew** (35), were sent by Veitch's Exeter nursery to explore the American continents and the Far East. Mid-century, Joseph (later Sir Joseph) Hooker's Himalayan travels were introducing ever increasing numbers of rhododendrons – a species that had appeared in this country only in the first decade of the century. Their introduction inspired some of the more adventuresome among the gardeners to hybridize these new species. Samuel Smith at **Penjerrick** (45) and Richard Gill at Tremough (now the main campus of the Combined Universities in Cornwall) were the most notable of these.

The 'acclimatization of exotics' was another early enthusiasm. In 1837, George Croker Fox of Grove Hill, Falmouth, who had a reputation for growing oranges, lemons and bananas in the open, won the Banksian Medal of the Royal Horticultural Society of Cornwall for a list of newly introduced plants, while Augustus Smith at **Tresco** (1), encouraged by the unique climate on the Isles of Scilly, was beginning to grow pelargoniums, mesembryanthemums and agaves in the open.

The Royal Horticultural Society of Cornwall was founded in 1832, but had run out of steam by 1861. However, the inauguration of a Cornwall Daffodil and Spring Flower Society in 1867 by J.C.

Williams of **Caerhays** (61), and his cousin P.D. Williams of Lanarth, arose from the new commercial sales of narcissus begun on the Isles of Scilly. The interest in daffodil-breeding was shared by George Johnstone of **Trewithen** (56) and others.

By the end of the 19th century, horticulture and the collection of vast numbers of plants had displaced the grand designs of the 18th century. J.C. Williams demonstrated his passion for new species by sponsoring first the expeditions of Wilson and Farrer in China and the Far East, and later those of Forrest. In this generosity he was joined by George Johnstone and, in the 20th century, Edward Bolitho of **Trengwainton** (28), in financing the journeys of Frank Kingdon Ward. The discoveries of new camellias and magnolias, as well as rhododendrons, inspired a new breed of hybridist – no longer practising gardeners, but enthusiastic owners. E.J.P. Magor, a solicitor, at **Lamellen** (115) was among the earliest of these, followed by E.G.W. Harrison, a retired General, at the nearby Tremeer, both of whom were in the forefront of rhododendron breeders; while at **Tregrehan** (85), Gillian Carlyon produced new camellia crosses until her death in 1987.

The complacency of the Edwardian era was shattered by the onset of the First World War in 1914.

Many estates never recovered from the depletion of their staff by mobilization and death, and later by the need for financial retrenchment. Great houses were sold off as hotels, schools or hospitals, and their estates split up or neglected.

In the second half of the 20th century, climate changes – probably cyclic, since complaints of 'unseasonable' weather were common enough in the previous century – brought high winds in December 1979 and January 1990, and freezing gales in January 1987, which ravaged the protective shelter in many gardens.

In the face of such adversities, it is perhaps surprising that so many of the great gardens have preserved at least some of their former beauty, and have even, as at **Trebah** (51), **Heligan** (71) and **Trevarno** (30), been revived. Some fine new gardens, such as **Pine Lodge** (78), **Lamorran** (42) and **Bosvigo** (34), have been created, but the future will probably lie more with the many new gardens of an acre or two, designed on a much smaller scale, which have been planted and are being maintained solely by their owners, often in retirement, and which are themselves evidence of changing social patterns and ambitions.

## Times of opening

This Guide contains descriptions of over 100 gardens in Cornwall open at the time of publication, the majority of which have been, and may be expected to remain open for many years. A few smaller, private gardens, open for only a day or two annually, may change from year to year, when their owners, often retired or elderly, move or find opening too exacting, so it is always advisable to check in advance current times of opening. For this purpose, contact telephone, email and web details are given. Information about gardens for which contact numbers are not given, or that have opened since this book was published, may be found in the 'yellow book', *Gardens of England and Wales Open for Charity*, of the National Garden Scheme (NGS), or on their website **www.ngs.org.uk**. Several of the gardens listed may open on additional occasions for charities or local events, which may

# How to Use this Book

be advertised in the sources noted on page 244. Since hours of opening vary from year to year, opening times are given simply as 'am' (morning, usually from 10a.m.) or 'pm' (afternoon, usually 2–5p.m.), or 'am, pm' (morning and afternoon).

Please remember that most of the smaller gardens are private property, and are opened occasionally only through the generosity and enthusiasm of their owners. Do not assume that they can be entered at times other than those stated, or that on the larger estates a charity opening implies any public rights of way. When approached with consideration, most gardeners will be happy to share their experiences with you.

## Finding a garden

The gardens are grouped into five regions (each with a short introduction), and arranged alphabetically within a region. For purposes of cross-reference, they are numbered sequentially throughout the Guide. For each entry, the name of the owner (who is not necessarily the person who will answer enquiries); the address; contact enquiry numbers, and road directions (given in miles [ml]) are provided. In addition, the pronunciation of Cornish names is shown by a phonetic spelling, with the stressed syllable in capital letters – usually the last in two-syllable, and next-but-last in longer names.

Each garden has a grid reference – which applies equally to the Ordnance Survey *Landranger* 1:50 000 (one inch to the mile), and *Explorer* 1:25 000 (two and a half inches to the mile) – for the square in which it is to be found and may be named. The first two figures refer to the left-hand side of the square, the second two figures to the bottom line. In order to help you plan a garden visit, a 1:550 000 (approx. one inch to nine miles) map is provided inside the back cover of the Guide. Permanent brown road signs show the way to major gardens, and temporary yellow signs indicate gardens open under the NGS.

## Appreciation and official ratings

Where appropriate, garden descriptions give information about the history of the site and the persons who created the garden, so that the plants and features may be appreciated in a wider perspective.

Some properties have been graded by English Heritage (EH). In such cases, the **gradings** for the house and garden are given separately. There are three grades – I, II*, or II. Similarly, landscape **designa-**

12

tions are given for the localities – **AONB**, the national designation for an *Area of Outstanding Natural Beauty* – and the two local designations – **SAGLV** for a *Special Area of Great Landscape Value*, and **AGLV** for an *Area of Great Landscape Value.*

## Size, aspect, soil and climate

For most gardens, the aspect, climate, soil and size are given. Temperatures are divided into zones, dependent upon the average minimum temperature in February, the coldest month in Cornwall. They are as follows:

A   5–4.5°C
B   4.5–4°C
C   4–3.5°C
D   3.5–3°C
E   3–2.5°C
F   2.5–2°C
G   2–1.5°C

## Plants

Most gardens that open have their own plants for sale. These are distinguished from larger nurseries as follows: **plant centre** refers to a small 'nursery', such as those in some National Trust gardens; **nursery** signifies a commercial nursery associated with a garden, such as those at **Bosvigo** (34), **Pinsla** (79), and **Trewithen** (56). These may also be described as 'specialist' – such as the bamboo nursery at **Carwinion** (36) and the clematis and pelargonium nursery at **Roseland House** (20); 'wholesale' – such as the camellia nursery at **Trewidden** (31); or 'full-scale' – such as at **Burncoose** (6), one of Cornwall's premier nurseries. There is a full list of other nurseries, not associated with gardens, on pages 249–51.

Some gardens listed have special plant collections registered by the National Council for the Conservation of Plants

and Gardens (NCCPG). These **National Collections** are noted where they occur.

## Facilities

**Facilities** differ from garden to garden. A key to the symbols used is given on the flap inside the front cover. If a symbol does not appear, the facility is not available – e.g., wheelchair access – or perhaps not allowed – for example, dogs. However, enquiries may be made in special cases. It is to be expected that guide dogs for the blind will always be admitted. A few National Trust gardens have a Braille guide and scented gardens.

## Historic gardens

A supplement of important **historic gardens** that open only occasionally (pages 244–7), gives suggestions for obtaining information on opening times, which are variable, or announced only locally.

## Calendar

In order to find the gardens open at times convenient to you, the **Calendar** (pages 251–3) groups them in three sections:

1   Open throughout the year
2   Open during the season
    – usually March to October
3   Open only on one or two
    days, arranged by months.

Each entry is cross-referenced to the more detailed entries in the Guide.

## Note

The information in the Guide is accurate at the time of publication. However, gardens may change their hours of opening, and neither the author nor the publishers are responsible for any such changes, which may occur without notice.

The Isles of Scilly, although only some 28 miles out from Land's End, for most of their history led an isolated existence, often with little more than a subsistence economy. The mild, equable climate, usually frost-free, and rarely dropping below the 5°C necessary for the continual growth of vegetation, barely compensated for a landscape, never exceeding 45m (150ft) in altitude, barren of trees, quick-draining, short of natural supplies of water, and, except in a few places, not favoured with protection from the unceasing sea breezes.

The earliest settlement in historic times was an outpost of the Abbey of Tavistock on Tresco, which appears to have succumbed to marauders from the sea, to be replaced by a garrison on the island of St Mary's. The need to feed the military brought prosperity to the small population of inhabitants, but the peace following the end of the Napoleonic Wars led to a total collapse of the fragile economy, followed closely by famine. The Duchy of Cornwall, to whom the islands belong, were forced by public opinion to resolve the chronic poverty aggravated by the neglect of the Godolphins who were the lease-hold 'Proprietors'. As a result, the lease was transferred to Augustus Smith, a young philanthropist from Ashlyns near Berkhamsted, who sought an opportunity to put his ideas into practice. His far-sighted, though despotic 'reign' was to earn him the title of 'Emperor of Scilly'. By the time of his arrival in 1834, it is probable that many exotic plants had already been introduced. The Hottentot Fig (*Carprobotus edulis*), and other mesembryanthemums, echiums, and at least *Aeonium cuneatum*, all of which are now naturalized, most likely owe their introduction to passing sailors from the Mediterranean and Canary Islands. It was no doubt their attractiveness, and the potentiality of the unique climate that encouraged Augustus Smith to plant his own garden with tender species, once he

had decided to take up residence near the old Abbey on Tresco.

Later in the century, when the lucrative trade in early potatoes began to fail, on his suggestion, followed by William Trevillick at Rocky Hill on St Mary's, a box of the early daffodils found growing wild over the islands was sent to market with spectacular success. Some of these tazetta narcissi had been growing around the ruins of the Abbey, perhaps since the time of the monks, but the presence of 'Soleil d'Or', 'Grand Monarque' and *Narcissus biflorus* on The Garrison suggests that they may have been introduced by the soldiers' wives. 'Scilly Whites' were prolific in the orchards at Newford, the farm of the former Lord Proprietor's agent. The *Nar-*

# 1 ISLES OF SCILLY

cissus 'Campernelli' had been given by the captain of a French ship to Mrs Gluyas, wife of the resident Dutch Vice-Consul and one of the early 'Pioneers', in the 1820s.

The narcissus trade was developed by Algernon Dorrien Smith, Augustus Smith's nephew and successor, who made a trial of over 350 varieties, some 240 of which he introduced from the Continent. From 1885 to the First World War, the market in daffodils soared, exciting regular comment in the horticultural press, so that for a time every available piece of land on the islands was cultivated. To protect the fragile blooms from the elements, they were grown in small fields with high hedges, at first of elm, escallonia,

tamarisk and veronica (*Hebe*). In the mid 1920s, resulting from the experience of his son, Arthur Algernon Dorrien Smith during his expeditions in the Antipodes, the use of pittosporum became virtually universal.

Today a visitor is immediately struck by the profusion of exotic plants seen even in modest front gardens – agaves and aloes; perhaps the tall mast of a flowering furcraea; the black form of *Aeonium arboreum* and the spicy, scented *A. balsamiferum*; the rounded bushes of *Geranium maderense*, with intense violet-purple flowers; the white daisy flowers of argyranthemums, and everywhere naturalized cinerarias. Unusual wild flowers abound in the fields and on the cliffs.

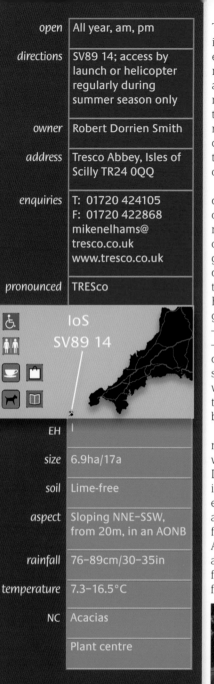

| | |
|---|---|
| open | All year, am, pm |
| directions | SV89 14; access by launch or helicopter regularly during summer season only |
| owner | Robert Dorrien Smith |
| address | Tresco Abbey, Isles of Scilly TR24 0QQ |
| enquiries | T: 01720 424105<br>F: 01720 422868<br>mikenelhams@tresco.co.uk<br>www.tresco.co.uk |
| pronounced | TRESco |

IoS
SV89 14

| | |
|---|---|
| EH | I |
| size | 6.9ha/17a |
| soil | Lime-free |
| aspect | Sloping NNE–SSW, from 20m, in an AONB |
| rainfall | 76–89cm/30–35in |
| temperature | 7.3–16.5°C |
| NC | Acacias |
| | Plant centre |

The Tresco Abbey Gardens are unique in the British Isles for their display of exotic and tender plants. This has been made possible by exploiting the favourable maritime climate, where frosts are rare and usually not damaging, and the humidity is exceptionally high. The major destruction is caused by high or chilling winds, especially of long duration, which have required the planting of strong windbreaks of pine.

In 1838 Augustus Smith took up residence in the house he had built to his own design, perched on a rocky eminence above the Abbey ruins, looking out towards St Mary's, and at once began work on his garden, which by his death in 1872 had arrived at substantially the form in which it is seen today. He at first planted collections of pelargoniums and mesembryanthemums – or 'mesmerisms', as he called them – over 50 varieties of each, and later obtained plants from distant parts. His sister, Mrs Frances Marchant, a talented water-colourist, painted 51 sheaves of the many exotic flowers, which have been reproduced as postcards.

Augustus was succeeded by his nephew Thomas Algernon Dorrien, who adopted the name of Smith. Despite being at first inexperienced in horticulture, he applied himself to enhancing and extending the plantings, although he is perhaps better known for his work with daffodils. His son Arthur Algernon, who had botanised in Australia and New Zealand before taking over from his father in 1918, widened the range of plants from his contacts there and in South Africa.

# 1 The Abbey Gardens

Today the 'bottle-brush' flowers of grevillias and callistemons from the Antipodes, and the cone-shaped blooms of the proteas and leucanthemums from South Africa can be seen along the Top Terrace. The banks above the Middle Terrace are crowded with great American agaves – which astonished the first visitors to Tresco – and aloes, the smaller African equivalent, joined by the bizarre, almost horizontal, long red-stemmed flowers of the beschornerias, while everywhere are varieties of aeoniums endemic to the Canary Islands.

# 1 The Abbey Gardens (continued)

The icy gales of 1989 wreaked havoc in the garden, but most of the great cycad palms and some metrosideros trees miraculously survived or have regenerated. The damaged western end of the garden has been rejuvenated by a new, half-acre (0.20ha), Mediterranean Garden to a prize-winning design by Carey Duncan-Haouach. Other recent additions are sculptures of the children of Robert Dorrien Smith, and a Gaia by David Wynne.

| | |
|---|---|
| open | At all times |
| directions | 1ml from Hugh Town along the Strand and Telegraph Rd; at a sharp bend take path straight ahead |
| owners | Community Garden |
| location | nr Longstone Terrace, St Mary's, IOS |
| enquiries | T: 01720 422404, or 01720 422153 |
| pronounced | Crake Dew |

IoS
SV91 11

| | |
|---|---|
| size | 0.6ha/1.5a |
| soil | Lime-free |
| altitude | 30m, in an AONB |
| rainfall | 76–89cm/30–35in |
| temperature | 7–16°C |

This community garden – the inspiration of June and Richard Lethbridge in 1986 – continues to be planted and maintained by volunteers. It has been created on several levels in an old ram pit quarry – 'ram' being a local clayey earth used to make roads and paths. The garden is sheltered from damaging east winds, so that it is possible to grow a variety of sub-tropical plants, shrubs and trees. Among these will be found a palm – *Phoenix canariensis* – and cordylines, an albizia, *Acacia retinoides*, eucalyptus and the tree fern *Dicksonia antarctica*, as well as agaves and furcraeas. This is a tranquil spot, with seats to relax in peace and quiet to enjoy the flowering of multitudes of daffodils in the spring, pelargoniums in the summer, or belladonnas and nerines in the autumn.

## 2 Carreg Dhu

| | |
|---|---|
| open | At all times |
| directions | In summer, daily launch services to the inhabited islands – St Mary's, St Agnes, St Martin's, Tresco and Bryher, and regular trips around the uninhabited islands |
| address | Isles of Scilly Tourist Board, Wesleyan Chapel, Well Lane, St Mary's TR21 0JD |
| enquiries | T: 01720 422536<br>F: 01720 423782<br>tic@scilly.gov.uk<br>www.simplyscilly.co.uk |

IoS

Flowers abound everywhere – in front gardens; on roadsides; in fields, and in the wild. In the centre of Hugh Town, **St Mary's**, the little gardens of the houses around the Park are bright in summer with the day-glow colours of the mesembryanthemums, the succulent leaves of aeoniums, and the various coloured geraniums. A stroll around the Garrison passes large formal gardens, luxuriant with hydrangeas, hebes and phormiums; the cottagey garden of Veronica Lodge ablaze with tender plants, and informal wayside beds full of sub-tropical plants – the battery opposite Newman House glowing in summer with an unbelievable mantle of wild *Sedum acre*, lampranthus and cineraria, all self-sown. In the centre of the island, the favoured climate of Holy Vale, once celebrated for its produce, now sports phoenix palms, trachycarpus and cordylines, with phormiums, echiums and furcraeas, as if on some Mediterranean shore.

On **Tresco**, the Island Hotel has a large garden, and there are woodlands. In the 'off' islands there is perhaps less formal cultivation, but so many of the more unusual plants, such as the aeoniums, echiums, lampranthus and 'mesems' have become naturalized that there is scarcely need for gardeners. The visitor may be surprised to find agapanthus, libertia, and the belladonna lily growing wild. *Gladiolus byzantinus*, known as 'Whistling Jacks', are common. There is no end to the wild flowers, but mention may be made of the old bulb fields where ixias – relics of former flower-crops – may still survive, among the striking golden corn marigold *Chrysanthemum segetum*, known locally as 'Bothams', and the tender succulent 'Bermuda buttercup' – *Oxalis pes-caprae*.

## Penzance and St Ives

The landscape of the extreme west of Cornwall, and the old hundred of Penwith, already denuded of trees before historic times, is a patchwork of small, prehistoric or 'Celtic' fields, scarred by mining. Only in the valleys running down to the sea, such as **Trewoofe** (32) at Lamorna, could the planting of trees and gardens be attempted successfully.

The principal fishing harbours grew up on the south coast at Mousehole and Newlyn, and on the north coast at St Ives, where in the narrow streets and alleys, 'the abominable stench' of pilchards once 'assailed the nostrils'. Here little gardens now glow over a long period with the vivid colours of mesembryanthemums, fuchsias and pelargoniums. Penzance eventually emerged as the main port and market centre, receiving its charter as a borough in 1614, and becoming the coinage town for assaying tin and copper in 1663. By the turn of the 19th century, when the Napoleonic wars had made overseas travel impossible, the borough, with its exceptionally mild climate, took on a new lease of life as 'the Montpellier of England', becoming prosperous enough for rich merchants and lawyers to build handsome villas such as **Morrab** (13) and **Penlee** (16) in town, or to erect their mansions, like the Bolithos at **Trengwainton** (28) and **Trewidden** (31), higher up around the perimeter, facing the sea, and typically orientated towards **St Michael's Mount** (22).

*(See gardens 4, 13, 16, 22, 25, 28, 29, 31, 32.)*

## Hayle and Helston

Hayle, not unreasonably, has been described as the 'cradle of the industrial revolution'. In the 1750s a number of adventurers from the Camborne district broke the monopoly of the Welsh smelting interests by setting up a Cornish Copper Company, which operated successfully until 1819, when it converted to an iron foundry. Of Hayle in those days a

contemporary wrote that as a consequence of

the fumes arising from the furnaces of Copper-house ... the glass placed in the windows of the habitations, after a little while loses nearly all its transparency. No bees can live within the polluted atmosphere, and in the gardens many valuable vegetables will not thrive.

With such an unsalubrious atmosphere, it is hardly surprising that the town attracted few wealthy residents.

Helston, in the hinterland of the Lizard, was granted its charter in 1201, at a time

Penzance
St Ives
Hayle
Helston
Camborne
Redruth

## 2 WEST

when the river Cober – cut off by the growth of Loe Bar in the 13th century – was still navigable. In these early days, Helston had no rival in the west nearer than Truro. The ancient estates of **Bony-thon** (5), **Godolphin** (10), **Penrose** (17) and **Trelowarren** (27), however, were situated at some distance from the town, and it was not until the 19th century that the prosperous citizens began to build villas such as **Lismore** (116), along the fashionable Cross Street.

*(See gardens 5, 7, 8, 10, 11, 12, 14, 15, 17, 18, 19, 21, 27, 30.)*

## Camborne and Redruth

The Camborne and Redruth area, in the eastern section of the ancient hundred of Penwith, and on the granite of the Carnmenellis extrusion, lies open on the north coast to the Atlantic Ocean. This part of Cornwall was one of the richest in mineral resources, and was consequently the most extensively mined district in Cornwall. It is no surprise that all of the great houses here, such as those of the Bassets at **Tehidy** (24) and the Williamses at **Burncoose** (6), **Scorrier** (23) and **Treg-ullow** (26), arose out of their profits in the mining industry.

*(See gardens 6, 9, 20, 23, 24, 26.)*

WEST

SX08 63

| | |
|---|---|
| size | Very small |
| soil | Lime-free |
| rainfall | 114–127cm/45–50in |
| temperature | Zone C |

Barbara Hepworth came to St Ives with Ben Nicholson at the beginning of the Second World War. Here, together with Naum Gabo, they formed the nucleus of an avant-garde school of artists. Before her death in 1975, Hepworth requested her executors in her will to consider 'the practicality of establishing a permanent exhibition of some of [her] works in Trewyn Studio and its garden', which she had purchased in 1949. This they were able to do, and the Museum, which from 1980 was administered by the Tate Gallery in London, has now become an integral part of Tate St Ives, which opened in 1993. The garden was laid out by Hepworth's friend, the composer Priaulx Rainier, in the early 1950s, with paths, pools and rock gardens. Hepworth was herself interested in the unity and relationship between sculp-

ture and its context. Here, in this tiny garden among palm, myrtle and cherry trees, camellias and ceanothus, we have the rare opportunity of seeing the works of this great artist in just the manner and setting in which she herself wished to place them.

The close-by **Trewyn Gardens** (below left), once part of the garden of Trewyn House, is now a public park, planted with tender trees and shrubs, and colourful bedding schemes. A sculpture *Megalith*, by John Milne, was placed in the gardens in 1976 as a memorial to Barbara Hepworth.

# 4 Barbara Hepworth Museum & Sculpture Garden

| | |
|---|---|
| open | mid-Apr–mid-Sep, Tues–Fri am, pm |
| directions | SW69 21, 5ml S of Helston on main A3083 Helston to Lizard road, turn L at Cury Cross Lanes by the Wheel Inn, entrance 300yd on R |
| owners | Mr & Mrs Richard Nathan |
| address | Bonython Manor, Cury Cross Lanes, Helston TR12 7BA |
| enquiries | T: 01326 240550 F: 01326 240478 richardn@ bonythonmanor.co.uk www.bonythonmanor .co.uk |
| pronounced | boNITHon, with a long 'i' |
| EH | House II* |

WEST

SX08 63

| | |
|---|---|
| size | 6ha/15a |
| soil | Alkaline and lime |
| altitude | 75–60m |
| aspect | S-sloping, in an AONB |
| rainfall | 89–102cm/35–40in |
| temperature | Zone B |

The estate dates back to the 13th century, but the fine main front of the present house was built in the 1780s, possibly to the design of William Wood, a pupil of Thomas Edwards of Greenwich. The house was described in the 19th century as being 'surrounded by considerable thriving plantations'. These, which consist mainly of beech and Monterey pine, had been planted in the late 1830s by Treseder's nursery, the paths surfaced with pebbles from Loe Bar, near Helston. More recently, the main entrance drive was edged with lawns and blue hydrangeas, but since the arrival of the present owners from South Africa in 1999, considerable development has taken place. The planting in the walled garden has been much extended by enlarging the herbaceous borders and creating a new, wide border between the swimming pool and lawn, with alliums rising above a froth of catmint. A gate at the farther end leads into what was once the working area, now laid out as an elaborate potager, where the newly planted vegetables make a colourful display. Beyond, through the lower gate, a vista opens up over a lightly planted orchard to Lake Joy, with an island and swans, and the countryside beyond. To the right of this lake, a second lake has been uncovered, which has been planted with ornamental grasses and tender South African species that have yet to mature. The new lake passes through a tree-fern and rhododendron dell, before emptying into a quarry pool, which is already picturesque, but will eventually be landscaped further. This formerly conventional garden has the potential to become one of the most interesting in the far west.

# 5  Bonython Manor

| | |
|---|---|
| open | All year, excl 25 Dec, Mon–Sat am, pm |
| directions | SW74 39, 3ml SE of Redruth on A393 Falmouth road, 0.5ml beyond Lanner |
| owner | Mr C.H. Williams |
| address | Burncoose, Gwennap, Redruth TR16 6BJ |
| enquiries | T: 01209 860316 F: 01209 860011 burncoose@ eclipse.co.uk www.burncoose.co.uk |
| pronounced | burnCOOZe |
| EH | House: II |

WEST

SW74 39

| | |
|---|---|
| size | 12.2ha/30a |
| soil | Lime-free |
| altitude | 100–80m |
| aspect | S-sloping |
| rainfall | 127–152cm/50–60in |
| temperature | Zone C |
| | Nursery: large, full-range, entrance free |

The first of the houses built by the Williams family, after James Williams emigrated from Wales to Stithians, sometime before 1654. The garden was largely created between 1890 and 1916 by Mrs Powys Rogers, a daughter of J.M. Williams of **Caerhays** (61). Hamilton Davey, the Cornish botanist, described her as

> A genuine lover of gardening …
> For correctness in the massing of plants, Burncoose can be cited as an object-lesson, every plant introduced into the garden being placed in position with some definite object in view.

He also remarked on her collections of 'rare Alpine flora', and bamboos. The garden subsequently suffered neglect during the Second World War, and was damaged by a freak storm in December 1979. In 1984, however, the former Southdown Nursery, which is now producing a vast range of ornamental and exotic plants, moved here from Redruth to take a central place on the estate, occupying the walled garden.

The private entrance to the property is now separated, rising from the lodge along a drive lined with camellias, rhododendrons, and many other trees and shrubs. Further south, from this point edged with fine stone kerbs, it becomes one of the paths through the main plant collection to the west of the

# ⑥ Burncoose Garden & Nurseries

house, in front of which a lawn with a sundial in its centre slopes gently to a stone ha-ha. Beyond this is a pond surrounded by Japanese maples. Along the perimeter are mature trees, some 150 years old, including Holm and Lucombe oaks, and a large Monkey Puzzle tree, believed to be one of the tallest in England. *Magnolia spenderi diva* 'Burncoose' and the *Camellias* 'Burncoose Apple Blossom' and 'Monica Dance' were raised here.

| | |
|---|---|
| open | One Sun in June and by appointment, pm |
| directions | SW72 24, between Mawgan and St Martin-in-Meneague. From Mawgan turn L into farm entrance after farm shop on R. From St Martin turn first R. |
| owners | Louise & Matthew Robinson |
| address | Caervallack Farm, St Martin, Helston TR12 6DF |
| enquiries | T: 01326 221339 |
| pronounced | carVALL'ck |

WEST

SW72 24

| | |
|---|---|
| size | 0.4ha/1a |
| soil | Lime-free clay |
| altitude | 65m |
| aspect | In an AONB |
| rainfall | 89–102cm/35–40in |
| temperature | Zone B |
| | Plant sales |

An artist's garden, created by Louise – a painter and plant-lover – and her husband, Matthew – an architect – whose interests are reflected both in its structure and planting. The garden is better de-scribed as in compartments than 'rooms', since there are views as well as connecting links between the various parts. The entrance is through a roofed lych-type gate leading to the front of the house, facing an open 'pump-house' attached to one of the thatched cob walls that are a feature of this garden. From this point an old brick path forms the spine of the garden, at first straight through a pergola covered with wisteria, roses, and *Clematis armandii*, where the beds along the outside are planted with spherical mounds of box, underplanted with silver santolina. Through the pergola to the left can be detected a formal courtyard garden with patterned paving and a central vase between four upright golden yews. A cob summerhouse backs on to the pump-house. To the right of the pergola, an informal gravelled area faces a large mixed bed. Emerging out of the pergola, the path weaves its serpentine way through

a variety of features. On one side, two metal lattice 'thrones' overlook a rectangular slate tank, attended by a sculptured angel with a bird. On the other side, a 'beehive' pavilion looks in upon a circular garden, with a tall metal fountain at the centre, whose mobile petals are operated by the flow of water. This little garden is enclosed on one side by a cob wall with a gothick aperture and a sepentine tiled top, and on the other by a yew hedge. Entry is through the pavilion. This intriguing garden deserves to be seen to be appreciated.

# 7 Caervallack

| | |
|---|---|
| open | Easter through Oct (closed some Mons and Fris in low season) – phone for opening times and prices |
| directions | SW67 26, from A394 follow official brown and white signs to Flambards, located on the A3083 |
| owners | Mr & Mrs Douglas Kingsford Hale |
| address | Culdrose Manor, Helston TR13 0QA |
| enquiries | T: 01326 573404<br>F: 01326 573344<br>info@flambards.co.uk<br>www.flambards.co.uk |

## WEST

## SW67 26

| | |
|---|---|
| size | In 8ha/20a theme park |
| soil | Lime-free |
| altitude | 70m |
| rainfall | 102–114cm/40–45in |
| temperature | Zone B |
| | Plant centre |

The greater proportion of Culdrose was absorbed into the Royal Naval Air Station, leaving a residue that was independently developed as the Flambards Village. At first this was little more than a theme park, but as new attractions were added so trees, shrubs and displays of flowers were planted to improve what had originally been a barren site of bog and scrub. It came to be viewed by the owners as no longer primarily a leisure centre, but more a 'garden containing various attractions'. The site was transformed – the various structures softened by the planting of flowers, and the different areas separated with large trees and shrub hedges, which introduced an element of surprise as visitors turned corners. The roller-coaster now emerges from swathes of hydrangeas and hebes, and the go-kart track is surrounded by slopes planted with shrubs. One of the more astonishing features of Flambards is their mascot, 'Ferdi' – a huge teddy bear, built of golden feverfew, silver-grey antennaria, and red alternanthera. Hanging baskets overflowing with flowers abound, and Flambards has attracted many awards: the gardens have been voted 'Top Business Garden' by the local authority for 13 years, including 'Best Hanging Baskets'. A theme park may not at first seem to hold appeal for the horticulturally minded, but when it is known that Flambards employs a head and seven other gardeners, it is clear that the garden is no sideline. The greenhouses contain exotic plants – orange and lemon trees, and banana plants, all of which produce fruit. A new venture demonstrates the use of hydroponics to grow exotic species.

# 8 Flambards Victorian Village

| | |
|---|---|
| open | One Sun each in May and Aug, pm; other times by request |
| directions | SW65 45, from A30 follow signs to Portreath; on entering village, Fountain Spings is second L after school, with a brown sign |
| owners | Mr & Mrs A. Keast |
| address | Fountain Springs, Glenfeadon House, Portreath, Redruth TR16 4JU |
| enquiries | T: 01209 842650<br>F: 01209 842650 |

WEST

SW65 45

| | |
|---|---|
| size | 0.8ha/2a |
| soil | Neutral |
| altitude | Sloping up to 50m |
| aspect | N-facing |
| rainfall | 89–102cm/35–102cm |
| temperature | Zone C |

The remarkable Glenfeadon House was built by Lord de Dunstanville of **Tehidy** (24) as a wedding present for his son. It has been renamed Fountain Springs after the many springs that run down the slopes by gravity and power the fountain in a small pond at a lower level. The garden rises up the steep side of the valley in four sections. The first is entered through a conservatory to the rear of the house on to a lawn, where, near the house, are two aviaries containing exotic birds, and a cherry tree. In the second section, these smaller birds are joined by a pair of tame peacocks, named – since this is designed as a 'Biblical Garden' – Solomon and Sheba. There are various other features here with scriptural connections, such as an enclosed white 'bridal garden', where the pitchers are reminiscent of the Woman of Samaria. There is also a Calvary, and a Resurrection garden with scattered seats and a shelter for quiet meditation. Small plaques contain apt, mostly Old Testament quotations at the foot of plants, several of which have biblical associations – a date palm, two olive trees, figs, a Judas tree, and on the lower lawn a Cedar, perhaps from Lebanon. The third section has been planted as a mixed orchard, beneath which is a carpet of daffodils in the spring. The final section, which has yet to be developed, is a puzzle since it is reputed to have been a tennis court, yet today there are trees growing and springs flowing through it. A path runs up the whole length of the glen on which, near the house, a platform has been constructed to give a scenic view over the harbour to the sea beyond.

# 9 Fountain Springs

| | |
|---|---|
| open | Easter–Sep (enquire for times), estate (NT) all year |
| directions | SW60 31, 1ml W of Helston on A394 to Penzance, turn R at Hilltop Garage on to B3302. After 1ml turn L to Godolphin Cross, Godolphin House is 0.5ml on L |
| contact | Mrs Joanne Schofield |
| address | Godolphin House, Godolphin Cross, Helston, TR13 9RE |
| enquiries | T:  01736 763194 godo@euphony.net www.godolphin house.com |
| pronounced | g'DOLPHin |
| | House: I |

WEST

SW60 31

| | |
|---|---|
| EH | Garden: II* |
| size | Garden, in large estate |
| soil | Acid |
| altitude | 60m |
| aspect | Sloping NE, in an AGLV |
| rainfall | 102–114cm/40–45in |
| temperature | Zone C |
| | Plant centre |

In 1535, Leland reported that there are 'no greater Tynne Workes yn al Cornwal then be on Sir Wylliam Godalgan's Ground', and it was from the wealth of their mining that the power of the Godolphin family, and the grandeur of their estates, devolved. Sketches made in the early 16th century show Godolphin as a castellated tower-house. The present front, with its colonnades, was remodelled in about 1635, and although the house remained unfinished, the surrounding gardens appear to have been completed. The present forecourt had two pavilions at the outer corners, and an arrangement of trees designed for walks beyond the front court, in which there were statues. To the rear of the house, on the hill above, was a deer park, where 'slips' have been identified as deer-runs used for hunting. Pevsner, in 1951, believed he had seen the 'remains of quite an ambitious garden ... in the solitude which surrounds present-day Godolphin'. This would have been the 'Side and Pond Gardens', shown on an estate map of 1786 as nine formal plots with hedges and a grand central walk running east to west, with stew-ponds to the north. Part of this garden by the house survives in a residual state; the remainder being buried in an adjoining field.

A courtyard behind the stables, to the right of the house and accessed from within, is known as the 'King's Garden', but is not now planted. This is an important site as the only surviving Elizabethan garden in Cornwall, and has been the subject of extensive archaeological study as a prelude to restoration. It is a place of great intrinsic interest and atmosphere, often featured on television and in films. The wider estate, with scenic walks over the former deer park, is now in the care of the National Trust.

# 10  Godolphin House & Estate

| | |
|---|---|
| open | One NGS Sun pm in May, and to groups by appointment |
| directions | SW77 24, 1ml out of centre of Manaccan village. Down hill past Inn on R, follow signpost to Carne. House on R, yellow NGS sign, park nearby |
| owners | Mr & Mrs Mark Osman |
| address | Hallowarren, Carne, Manaccan TR12 6HD |
| enquiries | See NGS yellow book, or www.ngs.org.uk |
| pronounced | HALowarren |

**WEST**

**SW77 24**

| | |
|---|---|
| size | 0.6ha/1.5a |
| soil | Lime-free |
| altitude | 5m |
| aspect | In an AONB |
| rainfall | 89–102cm/35-40in |
| temperature | Zone B |

Set in a beautiful wooded valley bordering a stream. At its widest point, the house is surrounded by a cottage-style garden, where a pool opposite the house, fed by a stream, has been sown with candelabra primulas and other bog plants, to form a water garden. Among the surrounding trees are magnolias and a *Liriodendron tulipfera* – the tulip tree. The garden then rises up through the valley, where the grass walk is bordered with old roses, lilies and many unusual trees and shrubs. The impression created is that of a haven of cultivation snatched from wild nature.

Hallowarren has won first prize in the Kerrier Council Garden Competition for the Woodland or Shrub Garden (Southern Section) for several years.

# 11 Hallowarren

| | |
|---|---|
| *open* | One Sun Jul, am, pm |
| *directions* | SW71 12, from A3083 to Lizard, turn L signed to Housel Bay and Church Cove – 0.5ml L to Church, garden on L, yellow NGS sign |
| *owners* | Mr & Mrs Peter Stanley |
| *address* | Landewednack House, Church Cove, The Lizard TR12 7PQ |
| *enquiries* | T: 01326 290909 F: 01326 290192 landewednackhouse@ amserve.com |
| *pronounced* | LANdeWEDn'k |

## WEST
### SW71 12

| | |
|---|---|
| *size* | 0.6ha/1.5a |
| *soil* | Lime-free |
| *altitude* | 60m |
| *rainfall* | 76–89cm/30–35in |
| *temperature* | Zone A |

Formerly the rectory of this parish at the tip of the Lizard peninsula – the most southerly point in the British Isles – Landewednack House benefits from an exceptional climate, where lampranthus grows wild on the cliff tops. The approach to the house lies between two beds, one of ornamental grasses, the other with tender border plants, to confront a bed of exotic varieties clearly intended to make a statement that this is no ordinary garden. It contains a cordyline, palm, fatsia and melianthus, surrounded by aloes, agaves, echiums, aeoniums, lampranthus, and a white agapanthus. This exuberance is somewhat moderated as one proceeds past the small mounds of box leading to the front door, and large lawn before the garden front. However, a fiery herbaceous border along the far wall beckons the visitor to explore the treasures beyond. There are formal rose borders, and mixed plantings that include exotics, often fringed with bright annuals. The kitchen garden is also of interest, for its screen of sweet peas and border of agapanthus. A blue plumbago invites entry into the Victorian greenhouse, with large tomato plants. On the far side of a formal screened swimming pool, a stream has been used to create a water feature, cascading over rocks into a pool with water lilies. This is a flamboyant garden in a unique setting, overlooking the church and the sea.

| | |
|---|---|
| open | Daily, admission free; Morrab Library, open to visitors, Tue–Fri am, pm; Sat am |
| directions | SW47 30; entrances from Morrab Road or from Promenade via St Mary's Road |
| owner | Penwith District Council |
| address | The Morrab Library, Morrab Road, Penzance TR18 4DA |
| enquiries | (Library) T/F: 01736 364474 |
| pronounced | MORrab |
| EH | House: II |

WEST

SW47 30

| | |
|---|---|
| EH | II |
| size | 1.4ha/3.5a |
| soil | Lime-free |
| aspect | S-facing |
| rainfall | 102–114cm/40–45in |

Built in 1865–6 by Samuel Pidwell, a wealthy brewer, on open land running down to the sea, Morrab House passed eventually to Charles Campbell Ross, a banker who was MP for St Ives and four times Mayor of Penzance. In the 1880s, when Penzance began to extend, he moved to a site high above the town, and in 1889 the property was purchased by the Corporation for a municipal park, the house becoming the home of the Penzance Library. Reginald Upcher, a London landscape gardener, was engaged to lay out the grounds. His origin is somewhat obscure, but he may have been related to the Upchers of Sherringham Hall in Norfolk, a Repton garden. Whatever the virtues of his design, his knowledge of exotic plants appears to have been limited, and the reputation gained by the Morrab Gardens in subsequent years owes more to the gardeners and park superintendents than the original designer. By the early 20th century, Morrab Gardens were widely known for their unique range of tender trees and shrubs, such as eucalypts, myrtles, olives, and even bananas and oranges, many of which could not be grown in the open anywhere else in England, and fulfilling the prophecy of the *Gardeners' Chronicle* that

The new Penzance public park promises to give a great impetus to acclimatization ... where tourists may fancy themselves in the tropics or on the Mediterranean shores.

There remains a Victorian bandstand, and a pool with a fountain, although the old cast-iron shelter has given way to more comfortable quarters for the aged. Despite the vagaries of the weather, and financial constraints, the Gardens have retained their capacity to persuade visitors they have entered a strange and unfamiliar world.

# 13 Morrab Gardens

| | |
|---|---|
| open | All year, daily, am, pm |
| directions | SW55 36, follow A30 to Hayle, from St Ives/St Erth roundabout, then follow brown and white signs to Paradise Park |
| owner | Mr Michael Reynolds |
| address | Paradise Park, Hayle TR27 4HB |
| enquiries | T: 01736 751020 F: 01736 751028 info@ paradisepark.org.uk www.paradise park.org.uk |

WEST

SW55 36

| | |
|---|---|
| size | 0.8ha/2a |
| soil | Alkaline |
| aspect | W-sloping, from 20m |
| rainfall | 102–114cm/40–45in |
| temperature | Zone C |
| | Plant sales |

Developed in the grounds of Glanmor, a Victorian villa built by a wealthy industrialist during the years of Hayle's prosperity, Paradise Park is a 14-acre (6ha) site, opened in 1973 as a breeding centre for rare and endangered birds. It has developed into a breeding collection of international importance, and is now the base for the World Parrot Trust. The former walled garden associated with the Victorian house has been utilized as a garden setting for exhibiting a selection of the more attractive and interesting birds. Here pergolas and trellis-work have been erected to support roses and clematis, with gazebos for a leisured view of the garden and birds. Two of the special features are a 'Parrot Jungle' and a walk through 'Australian Aviary'. Paradise Park offers the opportunity to combine a garden visit with an enthralling exhibition of bird life.

# 14 Paradise Park

| | |
|---|---|
| open | Enquire for details |
| directions | SW58 28, turn off A394 at Germoe Cross Roads to Praa Sands. Pengersick is on R |
| owner | Mrs Angela Evans |
| address | Pengersick Castle, Praa Sands, Breage TR20 9SJ |
| enquiries | T: 01736 762579 |
| pronounced | penGERsick with a hard 'g' |
| EH | House and tower: I |

WEST

SW58 28

| | |
|---|---|
| size | Small |
| soil | Lime-free |
| altitude | 40m |
| aspect | In an AONB |
| rainfall | 88–102cm/35–40in |
| temperature | Zone B |

The description by Maton at the end of the 18th century, when Pengersick had long been a ruin, paints a more realistic picture of its condition down the centuries than is gained from its shape today.

About four miles from Marazion, and a half an one from the high road, towards the coast, stands Pengerswick [sic] Castle, of which a square stone tower, of three stories, with a smaller one annexed, and some fragments of walls are the only remains. The door, on the north, is machicolated [through which hot coals could be dropped on invaders]. The different apartments are now used as granaries and hay-lofts, but the wainscoat, which is of oak, remains perfect. This wainscot is very curiously carved and painted, and there are several quaint pieces of poetry inscribed on the panels. A winding stone stair-case leads to the top of the principal tower, which commands a good view of the surrounding country.

Pengersick should be described as a fortified manor house, rather than a castle. It was built around 1510 by John Milleton, who was married to Elizabeth Worth, the last direct descendant of the Pengersick family. The tower was added later as a sign of his power and influence in the neighbourhood, rather than as a defence. The actual plan of the original is a matter of conjecture, but a sketch by Borlase from the now lost 'inscribed panels' gives a general impression of a typical tower-house with a walled front court. This now constitutes the present terraced garden, although records of any earlier gardens have so far eluded discovery. Nevertheless, an arch has been reconstructed leading to a 'recreated Medieval Garden' or herbary, and a small 'Tudor Knot Garden' has been planted. There is a 'Resource Centre' with information about the site, and the Tower may be visited.

# 15  Pengersick Castle

| | |
|---|---|
| *open* | Daily, am, pm, admission free |
| *directions* | SW47 30, entrance on R past Public Library down Morrab Rd |
| *owners* | Penwith District Council |
| *address* | Penlee House, Morrab Road, Penzance PR18 4HE |
| *enquiries* | T:  01736 363625<br>F:  01736 361312<br>info@<br>penleehouse.org.uk |
| *pronounced* | penLEE |

## WEST

## SW47 30

| | |
|---|---|
| *size* | 6ha/15a |
| *soil* | Lime-free |
| *rainfall* | 102–114cm/40–45in |
| *temperature* | Zone C |

Land from the 'Lower Morrab' – a word which in Cornish meant the 'seashore' or seaward part of the parish – was conveyed to the prosperous miller, J.R. Branwell (of a Penzance family related to the mother of the Brontë sisters,) between 1860 and 1865, after which he began to build his house, perhaps to the design of John Matthews, town surveyor for Penzance. Along the east side it had a conservatory, and was surrounded by parkland of a quite different style from that at the **Morrab Gardens** (13). After the Second World War, the property passed into the ownership of the Corporation as a Memorial. The entrance is through a shrubbery, leading to the house, which is now a museum and art gallery. The walled garden has become the site of a small memorial chapel, framed with cordylines. The garden is laid out in small lawns, with beds containing a number of exotic species, such as the shrubby echium, and beschornerias. On the walls are various tender shrubs and climbers – fuchsias, bomarea, and *Asarina erubescens,* with the rare *Vallea stipularis* at the entrance. The parkland has been retained for the benefit of the public, chiefly as a recreation ground.

# 16  Penlee Memorial Gardens

| | |
|---|---|
| open | Estate at all times to walkers; house and garden private |
| directions | SW64 25, access from 4 car-parks: (1) from Helston 1.25ml along Degibna Lane past Nansloe Manor Hotel; (2) 1.5ml from Helston along B3304; (3) and (4) both about 0.5ml along coast road E out of Porthleven |
| owner | NT |
| location | Near Helston |
| enquiries | T: 01326 561407 lizard@nationaltrust .org.uk www.nationaltrust .org.uk |
| pronounced | penROSE |
| EH | House, bath house: II |

**P**

## WEST

### SW64 25

| | |
|---|---|
| size | 648ha/1,600a |
| soil | Lime-free |
| altitude | 60m to sea |
| aspect | On NE-facing side of SE-sloping valley, in an AONB |
| rainfall | 76–89cm/30–35in |
| temperature | Zone B |

The Penrose family became extinct, and in 1770 the estate was sold to Hugh Rogers, whose brother John extended his lands, in 1785 establishing a deer park. The new owners added elegant stables with a clock turret, and relandscaped the grounds to take fuller advantage of the prospect over the Loe Pool and the Degibna Woods on the other side. A bath house was erected in about 1837 (restored by the National Trust), and some ten years later a bridge was built over the river, clearly intended to act as a feature in the view, which, as Pevsner remarked, overlooks 'Loe Pool as if it were an artificial serpentine lake especially made as a vista for the house'. It was at about this time that the Helston Lodge was constructed in a Victorian Tudor style, but the Bar Lodge, built in 1895–8 by estate workmen to designs of the Plymouth architect G.H. Fellowes Prynne, was rather more elaborate, being adorned with a wooden balustraded balcony. This was intended to open into an impressive new drive up to the house, which was never completed.

John Jope Rogers, who lived at Penrose during the second half of the 19th century, had a lively interest in horticulture, and contributed several valuable articles to journals, recording the effects upon trees and shrubs of the bad winters in 1860–61 and 1878–9. He also announced the fruiting of the uncommon *Abies religiosa* at Penrose – believed to have been the first time in this country.

17 Penrose

| | |
|---|---|
| open | Apr–Jul, am, pm, by appointment |
| directions | SW74 16, along Lizard road from Helston (A383), turn L on to B3293 to St Keverne. About 2ml after Goonhilly Earth Station, turn R immediately before the garage. Take 2nd turn R, signed to Gwenter, then 2nd turn L. Poldowrian is after Penhallick and Pensongath |
| owner | Mrs P.S. Hadley |
| address | Poldowrian, Coverack, Helston TR12 6SL |
| enquiries | T:  01326 280468 vjhadley@talk21.com |
| pronounced | polDOWrian |

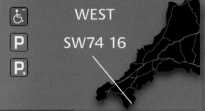

WEST

SW74 16

| | |
|---|---|
| size | 1.8ha/4.5a |
| soil | Lime-free |
| aspect | Sloping from 60m, in an AONB |
| rainfall | 89–102cm/35–40in |
| temperature | Zone B |

An almost indescribable wild garden along the very edge of the coast, not far from the southernmost point of the Lizard, Poldowrian has been created since 1969 along a narrow valley, where a stream runs down and over the cliff to the sea. Various pines – *P. radiata*, *muricata*, *contorta* and *maritima* – were planted to the west of the stream as a necessary windbreak against the gales. 'We have tried to make Poldowrian a blend of the wild and cultivated', the owner writes, adding, 'though the wild can quickly take over'! A pool was dug out early on at the top of the garden, and the clematis, rhododendrons, camellias, cistus and ceanothus in the garden can be seen from the coastal path below. There are prehistoric sites here – the remains of a Bronze Age round house, and a probable Mesolithic workshop, radiocarbon-dated to 5500 BC – and the owner's Museum of Prehistory may be seen on request, making a visit to this garden a unique experience.

# 18 Poldowrian Garden

| | |
|---|---|
| open | Phone for opening times |
| directions | SW74 29, from Constantine take Falmouth road to High Cross, turn R to Port Navas, garden 100yd on R. From Treliever Cross roundabout on A39 near Penryn for 3.5ml, take Mabe road past Argal reservoir to Lamanva crossroad, R to High Cross, L to Port Navas, garden on R |
| owners | Dan Thomas & Peter Skerrett |
| address | Potager Garden, High Cross, Constantine, Falmouth TR11 5RE |
| enquiries | T: 01326 341258 info@potagergarden nursery.co.uk www.potagergarden nursery.co.uk |
| pronounced | 'potajay', as in French |

WEST

SW74 29

| | |
|---|---|
| size | 2ha/5a |
| soil | Lime-free |
| aspect | N-sloping from 95m, in an AONB |
| rainfall | 102–114cm/40–45in |
| temperature | Zone C |
| | Plant sales |

56

A visit to the Potager Garden will gain entry into the early stages of an innovative and – for Cornwall – a unique project in process of development by a horticulturist and an architect. A 'potager' literally describes 'an ornamental productive garden', which is more usually seen as a parterre ornamented with colourful vegetables, with artificially trained fruit trees. Here, this garden is being designed along broader lines to demonstrate the beauty of productive gardening, both at the domestic level and in a wider perspective. The site had been used originally as a market garden producing flowers and fruit, but in the 1980s it became the 'High Cross Garden Centre'. This was taken over in 2000 for the Potager Garden, after many years of dereliction resulting in the invasion of bracken and bramble among overgrown trees. Great strides have been made in clearance, and in making a start with the project. The garden has been open for the Doubleday Foundation, and in 2004 will receive the Symbol of the Soil Association, both of which reflect the aspirations of the owners. Already students from the Falmouth School of Art attend for design sessions, in which they have created, among other projects, willow sculptures. A forge has been set up for metal work, and centres for craft and handmade furniture are up and running. Visitors will be encouraged not only to enjoy what they see, but also to learn how the ideas on conservation, energy-saving, and organic production are relevant and practical in their own gardens. This is an exciting new scheme set in a landscape that looks out over the Cornish countryside to distant hills.

| | |
|---|---|
| open | Apr–Sep, Tues and Wed, pm |
| directions | SW75 44, at Truro end of main street |
| owners | Mr & Mrs C. Pridham |
| address | Roseland House, Chacewater, Truro TR4 8QB |
| enquiries | T: 01872 560451<br>clematis@<br>roselandhouse.co.uk<br>www.roselandhouse.co.uk |

SW75 44
WEST

| | |
|---|---|
| size | 0.4ha/1a |
| soil | Neutral |
| altitude | 30m |
| aspect | SW |
| rainfall | 102–114cm/40–45in |
| temperature | Zone C |
| NC | *Clematis viticella* cultivars |
| | Nursery specialist: clematis, pelargoniums, etc |

The original house, dating from the 1700s, later passed to a mine captain, and was remodelled in 1847. Chacewater is in a mining area where the light, shaley soil conceals arsenic, and mineral deposits that can prove lethal to plants that root into them. When the present owners arrived in the early 1980s, the garden was overgrown, so after clearing the ground they began to improve the soil, philosophically reconciling themselves to the loss of those plants that became poisoned. When Charlie Pridham retired from the Merchant Navy, he and his wife decided to supplement their income by starting a nursery. By this time, the pond in front of the house had been dug, and the leaning *Eucalyptus aggregata* planted, which had been grown from seed. The beds behind the pond were then filled with an array of herbaceous varieties, mixed with shrubs used principally as supports for a collection of some 300 climbers, roses and honeysuckles, and especially clematis, of which some 150 varieties are grown. A long pergola follows the path down the slope to the gate, over which climbs the deep pink *Clematis* 'Dr Ruppel', and the white 'Marie Boisselot'. There are also roses – the 'Kew Rambler', and the fragrant 'Mme Alfred Carrière'. Sheltered in the greenhouse are scented-leaf pelargoniums, several varieties of passion flower, and a *Pandorea pandorana* 'Golden Rain'. The conservatory at the rear of the house, covered by *Wisteria floribunda*, contains the strongly scented *Jasminum polyanthum*, and the rose *R. chinensis* 'Mutabilis'. This upper garden contains some of the original trees, including old Cornish varieties – among them the 'Chacewater Long-stalk' apple, a curiosity that has fruits small enough to pass through the neck of a bottle, in which they would then be pickled.

| | |
|---|---|
| open | Garden all year, am, pm, enquire for restaurant, etc. out of season |
| directions | SW79 20, from Helston towards St Keverne on B3294, turn R on to B3294 to Coverack and follow brown signs. From St Keverne village follow sign to Dean Point, Roskillys R at crossroad in less than 0.5ml |
| owners | Roskilly family |
| address | Roskillys, Tregellast Barton, St Keverne, Helston TR12 6NX |
| enquiries | T: 01326 280479 |
| pronounced | treGELL'st |

**WEST**

**SW79 20**

| | |
|---|---|
| size | 8ha/20a |
| soil | Neutral to lime-free |
| aspect | NE-sloping from 90m, in an AONB |
| rainfall | 76cm–102cm/30–40in |
| temperature | Zone B |
| | Plant sales |

Tregellast Barton was first mentioned as early as 1311, and the farmhouse appears in the Tithe map of 1840. The Roskillys, a local family, came here in 1960 after the marriage of Joe Roskilly. Since then they have always supplied milk and cream, but like many other dairy farms have diversified. They have produced their well-known ice cream since 1990, since when there have been many developments: a shop and farming activities, and the 'Croust House' restaurant, with furnishings designed and made from their own wood by Toby Roskilly, and decorated with stained glass by his sister Bryn. There had always been ponds at Tregellast, but the present upper ponds were dug out in 1978 after the droughts of 1976, and ever since have been filled naturally by springs. The lower ponds followed in 1984–7. All are stocked with carp and tench. They have since been colonized by wild mallard, moorhens, the occasional tufted duck and many other birds, as well as dragonflies, butterflies and other insects. Near the lower ponds are old withy beds, originally copsed by fishermen to make their crab-pots. There has been a continuous policy of tree-planting, with the help of the Cornwall Tree Planting Scheme, so that well over 2,000 trees are now flourishing. Around the upper ponds are many indigenous trees – oak, ash, sycamore, alder, hawthorne and many others, but interspersed among them are rarer and ornamental varieties – walnut, copper beech, two varieties of chestnut, the balsam poplar beloved of bees, cherry, and eucalyptus. Tregellast won an award from the Cornwall Farmers Wildlife Group, and was joint second in the *Country Life* Annual Conservation Award 1984. These most attractive and rewarding ponds and woodland walks are freely open under the Countryside Stewardship Scheme.

## 21  Roskillys

| | |
|---|---|
| open | Daily Apr, May + weekends in summer with castle ticket. Castle open Apr–end Oct, Mon–Fri, am, pm.; tel for winter opening, |
| directions | SW51 29, 0.5ml from shore at Marazion by Causeway; or by ferry. Park on mainland |
| owners | NT and The Rt Hon. Lord St Levan DSC, DL |
| address | Estate Office, St Michael's Mount, Marazion TR17 0EF |
| enquiries | T: 01736 710507 F: 01736 711544 godolphin@manor-office.co.uk www.stmichaels mount.co.uk |
| EH | House: I |

## WEST

## SW51 29

| | |
|---|---|
| EH | Garden: II |
| size | 2ha/5a |
| soil | Lime-free |
| altitude | c.18m; Mount is c.22m |
| aspect | In an AONB |
| rainfall | 89–102cm/35–40in |
| temperature | Zone B |
| | Plant sales |

A residence of the St Aubyn family since John St Aubyn was appointed Captain there during the Civil Wars. The site of the earliest garden, which may date back to the time of the medieval nunnery, is on the south-east side, surrounded by 18th-century walls. It was described in 1833 by Thomas Rutger as then containing

> several sorts of fruits ... such as the peach, nectarine, plum, &c., with strawberries of the most delicious flavour; and there is a myrtle tree in it of many years' standing. Other half-tender exotics might, no doubt, be introduced here with safety.

Indeed, they have been. The rocky southern slopes have been extensively developed by the present Lord St Levan. These are the 19th-century terraces, with stone paths, steps, and irregular beds, stretching to the west from the walled garden, with a 'bower house' in a little wilderness out of view of the castle above, and some way along to the east. When Dr Borlase visited and sketched the Mount in 1769, there were plantations on the northern slopes, by which time the disused Civil War redoubts had already been planted out as gardens. There is a late-18th- or 19th-century ice-house cut in the rock higher up on the north side, and 19th- and 20th-century pigeon-holes built into the natural crevices. A grotto to the east of the summit, known as St Michael's Cave, was in use as a retreat during the 19th century, as it still is today.

22 St Michael's Mount

| | |
|---|---|
| open | All year, strictly by appointment only |
| directions | SW72 43, 1.75ml from Chacewater on Redruth road, turn L to St Day. Scorrier House on R |
| owners | Mr & Mrs R.P. Williams |
| address | Scorrier House, Scorrier, Redruth TR16 5AU |
| enquiries | T: 01209 820264<br>F: 01209 820677<br>rwill10442@aol.com |
| pronounced | SCORia |
| | House: II |

WEST

SW72 43

| | |
|---|---|
| size | 4ha/10a |
| soil | Lime-free |
| altitude | 115m |
| rainfall | 114–127cm/45–50in |
| temperature | Zone C |

Scorrier House was built and planted in 1798 by John Williams, grandson of John Williams of **Burn-coose** (6), who was described as 'one of the most extensive and most successful managers of mines, as well as adventurers, the county ever produced'. The house once contained a unique collection of minerals, but the gardens were to become even more celebrated, since their gardener William Lobb (1809–63), who on their recommendation became a plant collector for Veitch's nursery, sent back plants and seed from his expeditions, which included *Fitzroya plicata* (1849), *Sequoiadendron giganteum*

(1853) – of which there was once an avenue at Scorrier – and *Thuja plicata* (1853). The Pinetum in a 2.5 acre (1ha) walled garden, where the collection is planted, therefore forms one of the more important features of the garden. There also survives what was described in 1881 as 'one of the finest and best managed Camellia walls in England', 116m (380ft) long and 6m (20ft) high.

The present house was rebuilt in about 1862, after a disastrous fire, and the grounds greatly improved, retaining the lawned terrace with a ha-ha, 100m (328ft) long and one metre high, adorned by several handsome classical urns. Among the other features at Scorrier are a fine conservatory, which has been restored; a Folly Dairy, and a Quartz Grotto garden, with formal rose arches. A circular quatrefoil knot garden with a sundial in the centre, surrounded by beech hedging, was planted in 1989.

**WEST**

**SW64 43**

| | |
|---|---|
| size | 405ha/1,000 acres+ |
| soil | Lime-free |
| altitude | c.85–60m |
| aspect | NW- and SE-sloping, in an AONB |
| rainfall | 102–114cm/40–45in |
| temperature | Zone C |

Although now sadly decayed, Tehidy – a Domesday manor – had been included among the ten Cornish gardens in Loudon's gazetteer of 1822. The manor had come by marriage to the Bassets in the 12th century, but the mansion – to designs by Thomas Edwards of Greenwich – was not begun until 1734, as a consequence of the family's increasing wealth from mining interests.

With the house came the laying out of the grounds, principally the work of Lord de Dunstanville (1757–1835), who against the odds succeeded in raising spruce, larch, Weymouth firs and other species in the shelter of *Pinus pinaster*, which served as nurse trees and were later removed. Although his skill was admired, the design was not without its critics. A writer in the *Journal of Horticulture* in 1878 informed his readers that 'One would like to see more clumps, more grouping, more individuality in the features of the grounds themselves ... instead of a series of long interminable stretches of wide walks'.

In the 20th century a reduced income from mining, profligacy, and fire, resulted in the estate being sold, to become a tuberculosis hospital. Several interesting features have now been lost. There had been a statue of the Antonine (Farnese) Flora, and a leopard in the celebrated artificial 'Coade stone' – the only specimens recorded in Cornwall. There were extensive kennels and a dogs' cemetery, an ice-house near the lake dug in 1781, and designs by Nesfield for a parterre. The house is now sumptuous apartments, and 'Lady Bassett's Retreat' for meditation has been restored as 'The Gazebo'. The two pretty thatched *cottage ornée* lodges at the south and east entrances have survived intact.

## 24 Tehidy Country Park

| | |
|---|---|
| open | All year, dawn to dusk; admission free, donations to RNLI (St Ives) |
| directions | SW51 39 , leave A30 at roundabout W of Hayle on A3074 to St Ives. After Carbis Bay, entrance signs to Tregenna Castle on L-hand side |
| address | The Manager, Tregenna Castle Hotel, St Ives TR26 2DE |
| enquiries | T: 01736 795254<br>F: 01736 796066 |
| pronounced | treGENna, hard 'g' |
| EH | Castle: II |

**WEST**

**SW51 39**

| | |
|---|---|
| size | 29ha/72a |
| soil | Lime-free |
| altitude | 90–60m |
| aspect | NE-sloping |
| rainfall | 114–127cm/45–50in |
| temperature | Zone C |
| | Plant sales |

The 'Castle' was built in 1774 on the heights above St Ives Bay for Samuel Stephens, an opulent merchant, by Daniel Freeman, master builder of Penryn, probably to the designs of John Wood of Bath. It evoked from the 'elegant' Richard Warner of Bath no more than faint praise – 'this stile [sic] of architecture may in general be pronounced as little less than absurd when adopted in modern mansions,' he wrote, yet he allowed that it might hold out 'the semblance of defensive strength, which in fact it does not possess.' Until recently, none have been found to praise the grounds except John Betjeman, who thought it 'a splendidly landscaped park with vistas of sea and head-lands to the north and east ... which not even golf greens and tennis courts can destroy.' After 100 years, even the Stephens family tired of it, selling it to the directors of the Great Western Railway (GWR) in 1877, to become a five-star flagship hotel for their highly publicized 'Cornish Riviera' express – a name probably suggested by the Riviere dunes across the bay where, legend has it, the sands had buried the castle of King Harold. The original house has been extended beyond recognition, and, after the demise of the GWR, the hotel went into decline. The present owners are the first to turn their attention to the garden as well as the house. Since 1996, the walled garden has been laid out to a design by Chelsea gold medallist John Moreland of Penzance, and planted luxuriantly with palms, bananas, and other exotic species, edged with neatly clipped box. Work is progressing on a new water feature.

## 25 Tregenna Castle

| | |
|---|---|
| open | On request |
| directions | SW72 43, 1.75ml from Chacewater on Redruth road, turn L to St Day. On R after Scorrier |
| owner | James Williams |
| address | Tregullow, Scorrier, Redruth TR16 5AY |
| enquiries | T:  01209 820775 jpw.tregullow@ btopenworld.com |
| pronounced | treGULLo |
| EH | House: II |

**WEST**

**SW72 43**

| | |
|---|---|
| size | 6ha/15a |
| soil | Lime-free |
| altitude | 105–85m |
| aspect | E-facing slope |
| rainfall | 114–127cm/45–50in |
| temperature | Zone C |
| | Plant sales |

The classical style house with a fine Victorian conservatory was built in 1826 for William (after 1866 Sir William) Williams on his marriage, but has been altered and reduced in size. To the rear is an unusual ice-house, in the form of a tunnel. The park on the north is separated from the house by a low granite balustrade. The principal entrance lies to the south, where there is a small lodge with gate-piers on which, the story goes, a note was once found affixed, which read:

> Pray, Sir Billy, do not weep.
> We've stolen one of your fat sheep.
> For you are rich and we are poor,
> And when that's gone we'll come for more.

There are two walled gardens to the south-east, cut into the valley side, one of which is an unusual oval shape. The grounds consist principally of a wooded valley with sheltered slopes, planted with many fine trees, of which perhaps the most notable is the

*Saxegotha conspicua*, Prince Albert's Yew, introduced in 1847 by William Lobb, who had been gardener in the neighbouring **Scorrier House** (23). The extensive shrubberies, as is common in Cornwall, are mainly planted with rhododendrons and camellias, with some acers and magnolias. One of the more striking features of Tregullow was the yew walks, one of which is still intact. Tregullow, like other Cornish gardens, suffered neglect during and after the Second World War, but since the 1970s there has been an active programme of restoration and replanting.

# 26 Tregullow

| | |
|---|---|
| open | Apr–Sep, daily am, pm |
| directions | SW72 23, from Helston on A383 to Lizard, turn L on to B3293 to St Keverne. After 1.5ml entrance is on L at Garras |
| owner | Sir Ferrers Vyvyan |
| address | Estate Office, Trelowarren, Mawgan, Helston TR12 6AF |
| enquiries | T:  01326 221224<br>F:  01326 221440<br>info@trelowarren.com<br>www.trelowarren.com |
| pronounced | treloWARRen |
| EH | House: I |

**WEST**

**SW72 23**

| | |
|---|---|
| size | c.13ha/32a; extensive grounds + woodland |
| soil | Lime-free |
| altitude | Highest point 100m (house 76m) |
| aspect | Sloping N–S from highest point to creek, in an AONB |
| rainfall | 89–102cm/35–40in |
| temperature | Zone B |
| | Plant centre |

A Domesday manor, the first garden at Trelowarren was recorded in 1428, when it was inherited by the Vyvyan family. The house was remodelled by the architect Thomas Edwards of Greenwich in the new Georgian fashion, when the chapel was also decorated with fine 'Strawberry Hill Gothic' plasterwork. Later, the Pleasure Gardens to the south of the house were formed, and the estate separated from the unenclosed Lizard moorland by a ha-ha on the southern boundary of the woodland. Three walled gardens were enclosed: one, later known as 'Lady Vyvyan's Garden', was built immediately west of the north wing, utilizing stone salvaged from the fire at the old mansion of Nanswhyden, in the walls of which were placed glazed Gothick 'folly' windows, with a turret folly at one corner; another was intended as a botanic garden, where plants were to be arranged according to the systems of Linnaeus and Decandolle, with a central 'temple' for use as a library, although it is not known how far this project progressed. There are formal lawns around the house, with wide granite steps, leading up to the raised walk and pleasure gardens. Here there is a mount over 50ft (15.25m) in height, making it the highest point on the Lizard, which was known as 'Three Seas Point', since from it the Channel could be seen on both sides of the Lizard, as well as the Atlantic. Today, because of the growth of trees, only the latter is visible. Until her death in 1976, Trelowarren was well known from the writings of Lady C.C. (Clara) Vyvyan, a daughter of Mrs Powys Rogers (see **Burncoose** [6]).

| | |
|---|---|
| *open* | Mid-Feb–end Oct, Sun–Thur (+ Good Fri) am, pm |
| *directions* | SW44 31, 2ml NW of Penzance, 0.5ml W of Heamoor, Penzance–Morvah road (B3312), 0.5ml off St Just road (A3071) |
| *owners* | NT |
| *address* | Trengwainton, Penzance TR20 8RZ |
| *enquiries* | T:  01736 362297 or 01637 875404<br>F:  01736 362297<br>trengwainton@ nationaltrust.org.uk www.nationaltrust .org.uk |
| *pronounced* | trengWAINton |
| EH | House, bothy, head gardener's cottage, kitchen garden walls II |

**WEST**

**SW44 31**

| | |
|---|---|
| EH | Garden: II* |
| *size* | 10ha/25a + c.40ha/ 100a woodland |
| *soil* | Lime-free over clay |
| *altitude* | 120–75m |
| *aspect* | SE-sloping, in an AONB |
| *rainfall* | 114–127cm/45–50in |
| *temperature* | Zone C |

| | |
|---|---|
| | Plant centre |

A former residence of the Cornish Arundell family, but the landscaping is attributed to Sir Rose Price, of Penzance stock, who had made a fortune in Jamaica planting sugar. Under the direction of a Mr George Brown, he laid out plantations of conifers with elm, oak, ash and beech; dug three pools; constructed an ice-house; formed a terrace; built lodges, and created the nine walled gardens with ramped beds, which remain a feature today.

The estate, owing to family differences, did not pass to Price's son, and was eventually sold to Thomas Simon Bolitho, who enlarged the house and replaced Price's drive with the present carriageway. In 1925 Trengwainton passed to Lt-Col E.H.W. Bolitho, who set about developing the garden, aided by his cousins, the Williams of **Caerhays** (61) and Lanarth, and Canon Boscawen of Ludgvan. When George Johnstone of **Trewithen** (56) and Lawrence Johnstone of Hidcote, Gloucestershire, offered him a share in Frank Kingdon Ward's expedition to Assam and Burma in 1927–8, he readily accepted. His head gardener, Alfred Creek, became an expert in raising the seed sent by Ward, and in hybridizing rhododendrons, which were planted along the old drive. In the 1950s, George Hulbert planted a stream garden along the new drive with meconopsis, skunk cabbage, primulas and other bog plants, and the walled garden became a haven for the more tender plants, among them styrax, eucryphia, stewartia, and *Clianthus puniceus* – the 'Lobster Claw'.

In 1961 Sir Edward Bolitho received the coveted VMH from the RHS, and gave the estate to the National Trust.

28 **Trengwainton**

| | |
|---|---|
| open | from 1st Sun in Aug, daily until 31 Aug, pm |
| directions | SW45 29, take Land's End turning on A30 roundabout W of Penzance, after c.0.5ml turn R to Trereife |
| owner | T.C. Le Grice |
| address | Trereife, Penzance TR20 8TJ |
| enquiries | T:  01736 362750<br>F:  01736 362750 |
| pronounced | TREEVE |
| EH | House: II* |

## WEST

## SW45 29

| | |
|---|---|
| size | Garden, in parkland 5.5ha/13.5a |
| soil | Lime-free |
| altitude | 50–30m |
| aspect | SE-sloping |
| rainfall | 114–127cm/45–50in |
| temperature | Zone C |
| | Plant sales |

A fine house of the Nicholls family, who were there before the reign of Elizabeth I. Early in the 19th century the last male member of the family died at a young age, and his mother married the Revd Charles Valentine Le Grice, the boy's tutor, who became a minister of St Mary's Church, Penzance. Their son inherited the estate, which has since been the home of the Le Grice family. The last Mrs Nicholls came from the Usticke family (pronounced 'yewstick'). In about 1780 yews were planted, which now cover the south wall of the house, and which led her husband frequently to repeat the pun that there was '"yew" inside and outside the house'. A small park slopes away from the house to a lodge, but the estate was better known in the mid-20th century for its daffodils, grown by Charles Le Grice, who was well known in the industry.

Blight's description in 1861 is still recognizable today:

> The beautifully wooded grounds of Trereife … first attract attention; the roadway is here arched with a long avenue of noble elms; near its extremity it is crossed by another avenue … a few yards up on the right is Trereife House, almost buried in foliage; a yew tree is trained over the front of the building, giving it the appearance of a living wall of leaves … The walks and peeps of woodland scenery around this place are very beautiful.

The garden is being restored and a new parterre has been created in front of the house.

29 Trereife

| | |
|---|---|
| open | Daily, am, pm; free admission to RHS members Nov–mid-Apr |
| directions | SW64 30, signed from Crowantown on B3303, 3ml NW of Helston |
| owners | Mr M. Sagin & Mr N. Helsby |
| address | Trevarno Manor, Helston, TR13 0RU |
| enquiries | T: 01326 574274 F: 01326 574282 gardencoordinator@ trevarno.fsnet.co.uk |
| pronounced | treVARNo |

**WEST**

**SW64 30**

| | |
|---|---|
| size | 2ha/30a, in estate of c.304ha/750a |
| soil | Lime-free |
| altitude | 75–c.50m |
| aspect | NW–SE valley |
| rainfall | 102–114cm/40–45in |
| temperature | Zone C |
| | Plant centre |

John Betjeman believed that the poet Pope stayed here in the 18th century 'as a guest of the father of Dr Oliver the biscuit inventor', with whom he certainly corresponded. The present house was remodelled in 1839 by George Wightwick, the Cornish architect, for Christopher Wallis Popham, who built the walled garden and a conservatory, backed by a Gothic folly cottage facing the lakeside terrace. He was also probably responsible for the yew tunnel walk, 165ft (50m) long. The estate was bought in 1874 by William Bickford Smith, grandson of the inventor of the safety fuse. He was himself described by Betjeman as a 'learned artist', and it is to his initiative that we owe the principal elements of the present garden. He extended the lake, adding the neo-Gothic boathouse, and created formal lakeside terraces, ornamented with bedding schemes, rose gardens, and herbaceous borders, interspersed with gravel walks, which have now been simplified and grassed over. A rockery with its grotto, pool and stepped mount, was constructed on a spot where Wesley is reputed to have preached, and above it, along the main drive, a pinetum was planted with around 120 specimens. In recent years, the lake has been further enhanced by the construction of a cascade. Other features are the sundial on the side lawn, and an Edwardian summerhouse on a bank above the front lawn. Beyond is an 'Italian' garden, with a cast-iron fountain; the garden has been redesigned recently, though retaining the mature camellias and reintroducing the statuary.

One of the most interesting gardens in this district, Trevarno has the fascinating National Museum of Gardening – the largest collection of gardening antiques and ephemera in Britain.

## 30 Trevarno Estate Gardens & The National Museum of Gardening

| | |
|---|---|
| open | Last week Feb–first week June, Tue–Sun, am, pm; also bank holidays |
| directions | SW44 29, take Land's End turning on A30 roundabout W of Penzance; after 1ml turn R into Trewidden, just before Buryas Bridge |
| owner | A.R. Bolitho |
| address | Trewidden, Buryas Bridge, Penzance TR20 8TT |
| enquiries | T: 01736 363021<br>F: 01736 368142<br>mail@<br>bolithoestates.co.uk |
| EH | House, kitchen garden walls: II |

WEST

SW44 29

| | |
|---|---|
| size | Garden, in grounds 15ha/37a |
| soil | Lime-free |
| altitude | 90–70m |
| aspect | S-sloping, in an AGLV |
| rainfall | 114–127cm/45–50in |
| temperature | Zone C |
| NC | 114–127cm/45–50in |
| | Plant sales; Nursery: wholesale |

The drive climbs some 150ft (46m), for most of the way between old stone Cornish 'hedges'. The garden began to gain recognition in 1889 under Thomas Bedford Bolitho, whose gardener, George Maddern, after 45 years in 'one of the prettiest [gardens] in the west of England' in 1894 merited an obituary in the *Gardeners' Chronicle*. Trewidden contains perhaps the earliest tin workings in the county, in which the Fern Pit exhibits 'probably the best grouping of *Dicksonia antarctica* (Tree Ferns) in the Northern Hemisphere'. The shallower pits, known as 'The Burrows', also contain tree ferns. Near to the Pit, in a hollow, is the Rock Garden, with a small pool fed by a waterfall, perhaps most notable for the nearby collection of erythroniums. Thomas Bedford Bolitho had also gardened in Devon, at Greenway House on the Dart (later the residence of Agatha Christie), from which he brought a plant of the Chilean Nut, *Guevina avellana*, later described by the *Gardeners' Chronicle* as 'probably equal to any other in the country'. There are still specimens around the garden. The North Walk, to the rear of the house, contains some of the oldest plants, including a *Magnolia obovata* planted in 1897 by Bolitho's daughter Mary, who married Charles Williams of **Caerhayes** (61). Trewidden was overshadowed in the mid 20th century by **Trengwainton** (28), but is still famous for its collection of over 300 varieties of camellias – from China, India and the Far East – and many magnolias, including 'Trewidden Belle' and the superb *Magnolia veitchii*, which is believed to be the largest specimen in the British Isles.

31 Trewidden Garden

| | |
|---|---|
| open | May, Wed; Jun, Wed and Sun; otherwise May–Sep, by appointment, pm |
| directions | SW43 25, take B3315 W from Newlyn, after 2.5ml Trewoofe is on R just before Lamorna turn |
| owner | Mrs H.M. Pigott |
| address | Trewoofe House, Lamorna, Penzance TR19 6PA |
| enquiries | T:   01736 810269 |
| pronounced | TROVE |

WEST

SW43 25

| | |
|---|---|
| size | 0.8ha/ 2a |
| soil | Lime-free (pH 6.5) |
| altitude | c.65m |
| aspect | In an AONB |
| rainfall | 89–102cm/35–40in |
| temperature | Zone B |
| | Plant sales |

Situated at the top of the Lamorna valley, Trewoofe House was built in 1913 by Ella and Charles Naper of the Lamorna School of artists, several of whom painted here between the First and Second World Wars. The present owner – Ella Naper's niece – began a new garden in 1975. The leat to the former mill pool (haunted, according to the antiquary Bottrell), crossed by a small bridge, offered an opportunity for the creation of an extensive bog garden, which is planted with a variety of primulas; many kinds of iris, astillbes and arums. Reclaimed granite has been used in the garden to create a series of rockeries, and there are many island beds containing New Zealand shrubs, and some azaleas, rhododendrons and camellias. There are also collections of euphorbias, hostas, hellebores, and iris. Hidden from view, the fruit garden has cordon and espalier-trained trees. A conservatory by the house is well furnished with wall plants. This is one of the most remote gardens in the country, and as with all gardens in the extreme west of the peninsula, wind and salt are problems endemic to the site.

## 32 Trewoofe House

## Truro

Truro owes its origin to its position at the confluence of four rivers – the Calenick, Kenwyn, Allen and Tresillian – and to the convergence of important roads from the north, east and west. Although until recently never the county town, it has gradually increased in importance through the centuries. The wealth of the town was based upon the coinage of tin; the weekly market; an annual fair, and overseas trade. By the late 18th century, the town had grown to become the social centre of Cornwall, with its own theatre, philharmonic society, assembly rooms and, in Lemon Street, town houses modelled on those in Bath. Like that city, it began to attract many residents during the 'season', who also possessed country estates such as those at **Carclew** (35), **Tregothnan** (120), **Trelissick** (53), and the oldest of all, **Enys** (114). In the area by the Quay there are still several fine Georgian houses, built for wealthy and prominent

Truro families:
the Mansion House, Prince's House, the Great House, and the Old Mansion House, some of which once had quite elaborately designed gardens. The building of the Cathedral for the new diocese formed in 1877, and the transferring of the Law Courts from Bodmin in 1988 has finally established the city as the County Town.

*(See gardens 33, 34, 35, 41, 44, 46, 49, 50, 53, 55, 56, 58.)*

## Falmouth

Truro was at first challenged as a port by Penryn, which received its charter as early as 1265. However, both towns were enraged when, in the 16th century, the Killigrews of Arwenack had both the temerity and the foresight to realize that Smithick on their estate, nearer the sea, had the potential for an even better harbour. Falmouth now has the distinction of being the finest natural deep-sea harbour in Europe, although it received

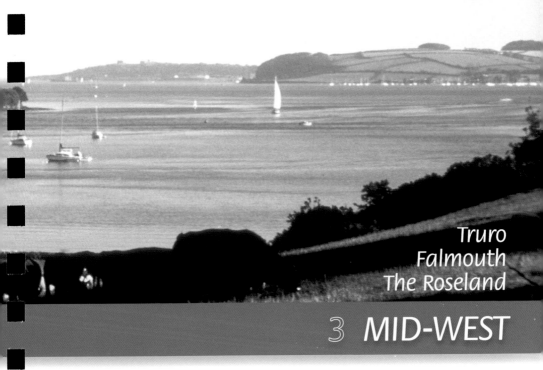

 Truro
Falmouth
The Roseland

## 3 MID-WEST

its charter late by Cornish standards, in 1661. In its first phase it was little more than a fishing port, but from 1688 until the trade passed to Southampton in 1852, it was the headquarters of the Royal Mail Packets, which brought with them overseas trade and travel, making Falmouth one of the principal ports of the county, attracting a variety of merchants and speculators. Among them were the Foxes – a west-country Quaker family from Wiltshire – who settled first at Bank House near Arwenack in 1759, opening their shipping offices along the road, overlooking the harbour. If not the most important family in Falmouth, they built, developed, or resided in at least 15 of the properties whose gardens received notice during the 19th century. George Croker Fox at Grove Hill became famous for submitting to the RHS of Cornwall in 1837 a detailed list of 223 tender plants that he was cultivating in the open in his garden, for which he received a Banksian

Silver Medal. Many of these plants were recent, but some orange and lemon trees had been planted much earlier in the century. Four other Fox gardens – **Fox Rosehill** (37), **Penjerrick** (45), **Glendurgan** (38) and **Trebah** (51) – remain among the finest in Cornwall.

*(See gardens 36, 37, 38, 39, 40, 43, 45, 47, 51.)*

### The Roseland

Today St Mawes is best known as a yachting haven, but it too was esteemed as a town in the 13th century, sending two members to Parliament, and becoming a borough after the building of the Castle in 1540. At **Lamorran House** (42), near the Castle, since the 1980s the most remarkable sub-tropical garden in the county has been developing, and the churchyard of the parish church, at **St Just-in-Roseland** (48), is a worthy rival.

*(See gardens 42, 48, 52, 54, 57.)*

| | |
|---|---|
| open | Daily, am, pm, excl 25, 26 Dec, admission free |
| directions | SW83 43, 0.75ml on R along turning to Malpas off Trafalgar roundabout at end of Tregolls Road |
| owner | Truro City Council |
| location | Malpas Road, Truro |
| enquiries | T: 01872 274766 F: 01872 225572 truro@touristinfo .demon.co.uk |
| pronounced | bosCAWN |

MID-WEST

SW83 43

| | |
|---|---|
| size | Originally intended to be about 9.3ha/23a |
| soil | Lime-free |
| altitude | At river level |
| rainfall | 102–114cm/40–45in |
| temperature | Zone C |

The need for an area for recreation in Truro was realized as early as 1864, when an appeal was made to the Town Council. However, little was done until the late 1880s, when Lord Falmouth donated the foreshore between Waterloo Quay and the Mill Stream, and the Duchy sold the adjoining foreshore between there and Sunny Corner for a nominal sum. The park was designed by F.W. Meyer, the landscape gardener at Veitch's Exeter Nurseries. In 1894 the *Gardeners' Chronicle* noted that 'The plan shows extensive areas of turf devoted to sports, and breadth and openness are not lost in a too great amount of tree-planting'. The completion of the scheme depended on reclaiming land from the river, which even as late as 1934, was stated as 'still in the making, only a portion at present being complete.' This slow progress, and subsequent developments, have somewhat modified Meyer's original plan, although there are colourful ornamental bedding schemes much in the position he intended, to which has recently been added a tall sculpture created by Jonathan Craig of Penryn out of the trunk of a dying *Cupressus macrocarpa*, which is as yet unnamed. The intention that the park should be used for recreation has been amply fulfilled by the provision of tennis courts, and cricket and football fields. From the foreshore there is a fine view of the Cathedral up the Truro river.

# 33 Boscawen Park

| | |
|---|---|
| open | Mar–Sep, Thur, Fri, am, pm |
| directions | SW81 45, 0.75ml from city centre: from Higher Town, near Sainsbury's roundabout, turn down Dobbs Lane; 500yd entrance on L |
| owners | Michael & Wendy Perry |
| address | Bosvigo, Bosvigo Lane, Truro TR1 3NH |
| enquiries | T: 01872 275774<br>F: 01872 275774<br>bosvigo.plants@virgin.net<br>www.bosvigo.com |
| pronounced | bosVIGo, 'I' as 'eye' |
| EH | House: II |

## MID-WEST
### SW81 45

| | |
|---|---|
| size | 1.2ha/3a |
| soil | Lime-free |
| aspect | S |
| rainfall | 102–114cm/40–45in |
| temperature | Zone C |
| | Nursery |

There has been a house at Bosvigo since the 13th century, but the present dwelling dates from 1780, and for nearly 100 years was the residence of J.R. Paull, a Truro solicitor, and his successors. The present owners came here in 1969, at first demolishing a Victorian wing, which isolated a fine conservatory, now home to a wonderful rose, 'Marechal Neil', *Pandorea jasminoides*, and many other semi-tender climbers. Their interest in gardening did not begin seriously much before 1980, since when the garden has gained increasingly widespread acclaim for its planting and association of colours. Wendy Perry has been responsible for most of the planting, and her husband Michael for the landscaping and maintenance. The walled garden at the east side of the house, made possible by the demolition of the wing, is planted with muted colours, mostly pink and blue. Beyond this is the 'Vean (Cornish 'little') Garden', in front of the Dower House, which has been quartered by pebble paths, the four beds reflecting each other, with the dominant colours gold and white with just a touch of blue. The slopes of woodland to the south of the house are planted with a host of spring treasures – not the rhododendrons and camellias one might expect in a Cornish garden, but bulbs and herbaceous plants to give a jewelled effect under the big beech trees. The display starts with snowdrops, a fine collection of *Helleborus orientalis*, epimediums, erythroniums and drifts of wood anemones. As a final surprise, tucked away in the woods is a 'Hot Garden', planted with reds, oranges and yellows, which will 'blow your socks off' in August. This is an all-season garden for the plant-lover.

| | |
|---|---|
| open | Apr–May, every Sun, excl Easter, pm |
| directions | SW78 38, on A39 from Truro turn L at Perranarworthal, entrance 1ml on L |
| owner | Mrs Pamela Chope |
| address | Carclew House, Perranarworthal, Truro TR3 7PB |
| enquiries | T:  01872 864070 |
| pronounced | carCLEW |
| EH | House: ruins II*; garden walls, terraces: each II |

| | |
|---|---|
| EH | Garden: II |
| size | Very large estate, with garden of 2ha/5a |
| soil | Lime-free |
| altitude | 85–25m |
| aspect | E-sloping, in an AONB |
| rainfall | 102–114cm/40–45in |
| temperature | Zone C |

Until the reign of Henry IV, the property of the Daunger family, in 1749 Carclew was sold to the 'great' William Lemon, who engaged Thomas Edwards of Greenwich to design 'one of the most ... elegant buildings [in] the county of Cornwall'. Lemon's grandson, Sir William Lemon, was principally responsible for laying out the garden and grounds, to be followed by his son Sir Charles, chairman and founder member of the RHS of Cornwall. He was fortunate in his gardener William Beattie Booth, a notable horticulturist, and later assistant secretary to the Horticultural Society in London. Sir Charles himself was a keen plant collector, encouraging the Packet commanders to introduce new plants; sponsoring Joseph Hooker's Himalayan expedition, and engaging as gamekeeper the father of William and Thomas Lobb, the great Cornish plant hunters.

Carclew was among the ten gardens in Loudon's gazetteer of 1822, and was frequently named in the great 19th-century horticultural journals. The main gardens are arranged around the 'Higher Pond' above the 'Wheel Pond', from which water was raised to the mansion, where many fine rhododendrons, such as *falconeri*, and the original Lucombe oaks are to be found. On the western slopes, the old formal terraces lead up to the present house, built in 1963, which has replaced the magnificent dwelling tragically burnt down in 1934, leaving only a romantic ruin.

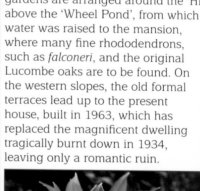

Lemon was succeeded by his brother-in-law, John Hearle Tremayne of the Heligan family, who continued the gardening tradition, sharing experience and plants. Although this once large and grand estate is now divided among smaller residences and farms, the greater part of the fine historic garden survives, owned and maintained as an intact whole.

# 35 Carclew Garden

| | |
|---|---|
| open | Daily, am, pm |
| directions | SW78 28, turning off Carwinion Rd S of Mawnan Smith |
| owners | Anthony & Jane Rogers, and NT |
| address | Carwinion, Mawnan Smith, Falmouth TR11 5JA |
| enquiries | T: 01326 250258 F: 01326 250903 jane@carwinion .freeserve.co.uk www.carwinion.com |
| pronounced | carWINion |

**MID-WEST**

**SW78 28**

| | |
|---|---|
| size | 3.8ha/9.5a |
| soil | Lime-free |
| altitude | 65m to sea |
| aspect | S-facing valley, in an AONB |
| rainfall | 102–114cm/40–45in |
| temperature | Zone C |
| | Nursery: especially bamboos. |

The estate was bequeathed to a younger son of the owner of **Penrose** (17), and the house was built as a residence for his son in the late 18th century. However, it was probably *his* son, Reginald Rogers (born 1854), who was responsible for the planting and design of the garden in the late 19th century, in association with the Fox family at **Glendurgan** (38) and **Trebah** (51) who were his cousins. It is possible that the family helped to finance various plant expeditions, from which they and neighbouring gardens profited. Indeed, the Carwinion valley has similarities to those at the Fox gardens, although it is longer and narrower. There are few changes from the appearance of the grounds in the early maps, although a former orchard to the south of the house has been replaced by two additional ponds, dominated by huge gunnera plants, and the walled garden has been grassed over. The present owner – a descendant of the same family – has planted camellias, eucryphias, and species rhododendrons, and in 1986 began a reference collection of some 160 species of bamboos, which are now one of the principal features, being distributed in clumps around the garden, with their names clearly labelled. Recently, the Camellia and Hydrangea Nursery formerly located at Porthtowan has transferred to Carwinion, where among its own specialities, many varieties of bamboo are available. The estate was donated to the National Trust in 1969, which also owns 20 acres (8ha) of woodland. The garden remains managed by Anthony Rogers. Teas are served in summer.

## 36  Carwinion Bamboo Garden

| | |
|---:|:---|
| open | All year, dawn–dusk; public park, admission free |
| directions | Melvill Road, Falmouth |
| owner | Carrick District Council |
| enquiries | T: 01872 224376<br>F: 01872 272239<br>smiles@carrick.gov.uk |
| EH | House: II |

## MID-WEST

### SX08 63

| | |
|---:|:---|
| size | 0.8ha/2a |
| soil | Lime-free |
| altitude | From *c.*35m |
| aspect | SE-sloping |
| rainfall | 102–114cm/40-45in |
| temperature | Zone C |

The town house of Robert Were Fox until his retirement in 1872, when it was sold to his nephew Howard, who was inspired by his experience of sub-tropical plants on his travels to design a Mediterranean-type garden. As early as 1880, the *Gardeners' Chronicle* remarked that the use of cordylines 'in a novel and picturesque manner ... form[ed] an avenue worthy of imitation'. It was, indeed, imitated along the road into Falmouth, which was planted and named 'Dracaena Avenue', ending just short of Rosehill itself. The popularity of this Mediterranean style of planting spread through the seaside resorts in Cornwall – as, for example, in the **Morrab Gardens** (13) in Penzance, opened in 1889 – and in Torbay in Devon, to promote tourism. In 1908 Charles Curtis, editor of the *Gardeners' Magazine*, wrote about Rosehill, then having reached its maturity – 'I cannot call to mind one [garden] in England, that is so altogether un-English as that of Rosehill.' The whole made up 'a picture of the character one associates in idle moments with a "Chateau d'Espagne"'. It was the family's intention that Rosehill should be given to the people of Falmouth, and to this end the greater part of the garden was donated as a public park, followed by the gift of the remaining grounds and the house, which was intended to become a museum. This the local authority felt unable to accept, and the two became separated. The house and grounds are now the School of Art; the remainder – the Fox Rosehill Gardens – has interesting exotic planting, especially the maintenance of the former banana grove – but is now reduced in size.

# 37 Fox Rosehill Gardens

| | |
|---|---|
| open | Mid-Feb–end Oct, Tue–Sat excl Good Friday; open bank holiday Mons, am, pm |
| directions | SW77 27, on road to Helford passage 5ml S of Falmouth, follow NT signs |
| owner | NT |
| address | Glendurgan, Mawnan Smith, Falmouth TR11 5JZ |
| enquiries | T:  01872 862090 F:  01872 865808 glendurgan@ nationaltrust.org.uk www.nationaltrust .org.uk |
| pronounced | glenDERgan |

MID-WEST

SW77 27

| | |
|---|---|
| EH | Garden: II* |
| size | 10ha/25a |
| soil | Lime-free over shillet with some clay |
| altitude | 70–10m |
| aspect | Sloping, in an AONB |
| rainfall | 102–114cm/40–45in |
| temperature | Zone C |
| | Plant centre |

Although perhaps the best designed valley garden in Cornwall, Glendurgan escaped notice in publications until the 1930s. It was purchased by Alfred Fox – younger brother of Robert Were of **Penjerrick** (45) – in the 1820s, who planted *Pinus pinaster* as windbreaks, to which 'he added a great variety of trees and shrubs, and made several orchards'. Glendurgan is remarkable in that there have been only three head gardeners between 1825 and 1960. The valley is larger than the adjoining **Trebah** (51), but without the same direct view of the river, although running down to the picturesque fishing village of Durgan. The Maze, begun in 1833, and modelled on that at Sydney Gardens, Bath, is the best known feature of the garden, but while the foundation planting may be attributed to Alfred, little more seems to have been done until it was inherited in 1890 by his grandson, George Henry Fox, a keen botanist. It is to him that we owe many of the conifers, as well as the fragrant and tender rhododendrons. George Henry died in 1931, and was succeeded by his son Cuthbert Lloyd, who, with his wife, increased the range of species and varieties. 'Many of the plants now at their best', wrote Michael Trinick of the National Trust,

date from this period, Asiatic rhododendrons and magnolias, cornuses, camellias, hydrangeas and eucryphias ... also some unusual plants – aloe, persimmon and evergreen oleasters.

# 38 Glendurgan

He added:

> Perhaps their part-
> icular contribution
> ... was their sense of
> restraint. Instead of
> planting up every
> corner, so tempting in
> Cornwall where plants
> grow quickly, they left
> glades and sweeps of
> grass and encouraged
> wild flowers to grow
> beneath the trees.

In 1962, on the bicentenary of the arrival of the Fox family in Falmouth, Glendurgan was donated to the National Trust.

| | |
|---|---|
| open | All year, am, pm; admission free |
| directions | SW80 31, entrances Melvill and Cliff Roads |
| owner | Carrick District Council |
| location | Melvill Road, Falmouth |
| enquiries | T: 01872 224376<br>F: 01872 272239<br>smiles@carrick.gov.uk |
| pronounced | gillingDOON |

## MID-WEST

### SW80 31

| | |
|---|---|
| size | Medium size |
| soil | Lime-free |
| aspect | S-sloping to the sea, in an AONB |
| rainfall | 102–114cm/40–45in |
| temperature | Zone C |

Originally 'Summerlands', Gyllyngdune was designed in 1828 by George Wightwick, a notable Cornish architect, for General William Jesser Coope, after whose death it became the residence of his son, the rector of Falmouth, who created a quite elaborate garden, with some parkland. The house is now in apartments, and the lodge, with fine iron gates, is isolated near Emslie Road. The remainder was purchased by the town in 1903 for leisure and winter gardens. The walled garden was then laid out as a lawn with bedding schemes, surrounding a central bandstand adjoining the Princess Pavilion. From this area, two sets of steps flanked by vases run down to a terrace, on which once stood stove houses for tender plants, recently demolished. From the terrace a path leads along one side of a quarry, from which the building stone for the house had been obtained, and which has been planted as a rock garden. Along this path there is a shell grotto with seats. On a prominence to the right, three slender blocks of granite form a primitive arch. There is a tunnel leading out from the floor of the quarry across Cliff Road – a later development – to a summer-house or gazebo which, because of crosses in the gables, has been wrongly termed a 'chapel', from which steps descend to the beach. Although the greater part of this complex is designated as a leisure area, it remains an interesting relict of a once grand Victorian private garden.

## 39 Gyllyngdune Gardens & Princess Pavilion

| | |
|---|---|
| open | Daily am, pm, admission free |
| owner | Carrick District Council |
| location | Kimberley Park Road, Falmouth |
| enquiries | T: 01326 315559<br>F: 01326 312662<br>www.carrick.gov.uk |

MID-WEST

SX08 63

| | |
|---|---|
| size | c.2.8ha/7a |
| soil | Lime-free |
| altitude | 30m |
| aspect | E-sloping |
| rainfall | 102–114cm/40–45in |
| temperature | Zone C |

The land for this park was presented to the town in 1877 by the Earl of Kimberley, as an ornamental recreation ground, which was then laid out by John Simpson Tyerman, formerly of the Liverpool Botanic Gardens, who lived at Penlee House in Tregony. The opening was announced in *The Times* of 26 May, and was considered notable enough for Edgar Thurston to include it among the select gardens in his *Trees and Shrubs of Cornwall* (1930), where he cited 15 trees. The Dracaenas (*Cordylines*) also received a mention in the *Garden* of 1880, and the *Gardeners' Chronicle* referred to plants submitted to the Falmouth Naturalists' Association exhibition in 1889. In recent years, a banana plant at the lower

entrance has been a notable feature. From the road, the bedding schemes are most prominent, but the other side of the valley is more wooded, and has a pond. The Earl of Kimberley (in Norfolk) had inherited the ancient estates of the Killigrews of Arwenack in Falmouth, by way of the Berkeley family, hence the un-Cornish names of both the Park and the Vale.

| | |
|---|---|
| open | One Sun Apr or early May, pm, or by appointment |
| directions | SW89 50, off B3275, by Ladock Church |
| owner | Mr G.J. Holborow |
| address | Ladock House, Ladock, Truro TR2 4PL |
| enquiries | T: 01726 882274<br>F: 01726 883580 |
| pronounced | LADock |
| EH | House: II |

## MID-WEST
### SW89 50

| | |
|---|---|
| size | 1.6ha/4a |
| soil | Lime-free |
| altitude | 50m |
| rainfall | 102–114cm/40–45in |
| temperature | Zone D |
| | Plant sales |

Built in 1820 as the rectory for the parish of Ladock, the house is well sited on a platform looking west over the valley and south over a wide lawn. Many fine trees have survived from these early times, standing proud with strong trunks, having resisted the heavy gales that afflicted Cornwall in the 1980s and 1990s. When the present owners came into residence in 1968, the house was somewhat dilapidated, and the grounds overgrown. Undergrowth was cleared, and trees thinned out, so that what was once dense woodland has become an area with widely spaced mature trees forming a high canopy above wide grass walks, sheltered by well-placed banks of the original laurel or aucuba. This plan has provided a splendid opportunity for the planting of rhododendrons, azaleas and camellias, which now form the principle attraction of this garden in springtime, when the ground is carpeted with bluebells. Many Cornish gardens grow these plants, but here they have been carefully selected, or have been received from notable sources such as **Trewithen** (56) and **Lamellen** (115).

To the west of the house is a meadow, in the middle of which grows a magnificent, wide-spreading, Turkey oak. A new garden is being developed on the far side of this field, seen from the house, and accessed around the side. Here and there new and striking trees have been planted, among which the birch *Betula jacquemontii*, with its white bark, stands out. A bank of hydrangeas of various tints provides a splash of colour along the side of the lawn in summer.

41  Ladock House

| | |
|---|---|
| open | Apr–Sep, Wed, Fri, + 1st Sat of month, am, pm |
| directions | SW84 33, 1st turning R after garage; signposted to St Mawes Castle, entrance 0.5ml on L |
| owner | Mr Robert Dudley-Cooke |
| address | Lamorran House, Upper Castle Rd, St Mawes TR2 5BZ |
| enquiries | T:  01326 270800<br>F:  01326 270801 |
| pronounced | LaMORan |

**P**

**MID-WEST**

**SW84 33**

| | |
|---|---|
| size | 1.8ha/4.5a |
| soil | Lime-free |
| altitude | 60–15m |
| aspect | SE-sloping, in an AONB |
| rainfall | 89–102cm/35–40in |
| temperature | Zone C |

The garden at Lamorran House was re-created by Robert Dudley-Cooke, who moved from his house in Surrey in 1982, bringing with him many rhododendrons, and particularly evergreen azaleas, of which there are 500 specimens, some of which had begun their life in Cornwall. The Japanese Garden with a waterfall and grotto was the first to be formed, and this was followed by work on the lower garden, which at that time was overgrown with blackthorn and brambles. Here a Mediterranean-type garden was created, surmounted by a small temple, and an Italianate pond. It has been necessary to provide shelter from the south-west wind from Falmouth, and scorching easterlies in the early year. Where protected, such plants as acacias, of which there are 12 species, callistemons, grevilleas, cassias, metrosideros and *Albizia lophantha* are flourishing. On a succulent bank there is a selection of agaves and lampranthus, with bourgainvillea growing on the wall beneath the temple. Travels in the Mediterranean region inspired an enthusiasm for palms, varieties of which have been planted throughout the garden – the more common, such as *Cordyline australis*, but also *Phoenix canariensis, Butia capitata*, and other rarer species. The various forms of yucca, dasylirion, beschorneria, and the succulents such as aeoniums and echeverias all add to the sub-tropical effect. The garden is continually evolving, and more recently has enveloped part of the former Riviera garden below. This fascinating and unique garden continues an earlier tradition in the acclimatization of exotics, most notably at the Fox family gardens in Falmouth at Grove Hill, and **Fox Rosehill** (37).

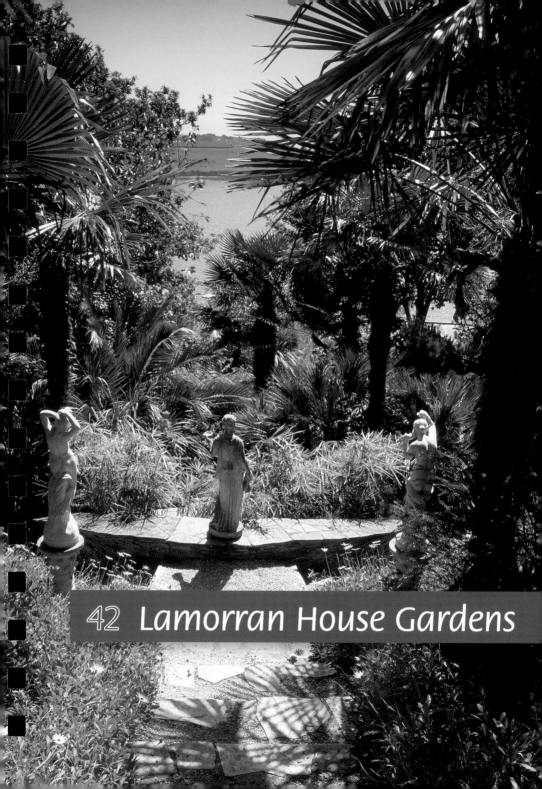

42 Lamorran House Gardens

| | |
|---|---|
| open | Daily, am, pm, entrance: donation to charity |
| directions | SW81 37, N out of Mylor to Restonguet Passage, entrance on R |
| owner | Mrs H. Hall |
| address | Lanterns, Restronguet Hill, Mylor, Falmouth TR11 5ST |
| | T: 01326 372007 |

**P** **🐕**

**MID-WEST**

**SW81 37**

| | |
|---|---|
| size | 0.2ha/0.5a |
| soil | Lime-free |
| altitude | Near river level |
| aspect | In an AONB |
| rainfall | 102–114cm/40–45in |
| temperature | Zone C |

Lanterns, through which a stream runs to Re-stronguet Creek, lies above the Pandora Inn. This is a plantsman's garden, begun in 1966, with a wide-ranging collection of species and varieties, both for the waterside and dry areas. By reason of its position it is possible to grow tender plants such as *Parochetus communis*, and the *Salvias elegans* 'Scarlett Pineapple' and *guarantica* in the open all year round. Alpines, always unreliable in the damp Cornish climate, are rarely attempted, but here *Soldanella villosa*, which is notoriously difficult to flower, flourishes. More intensive cultivation is made possible by the use of the two heated greenhouses, and a conservatory.

43 Lanterns

| | |
|---|---|
| open | One Sun each, pm, April, May |
| directions | SW89 50, on R entering Ladock from Tresillian on B3275. Park in Falmouth Arms or parish hall, with permission |
| owners | Mr & Mrs Michael Cole |
| address | Nansawsan House, Ladock, Truro TR2 4PW |
| enquiries | T: 01726 882392 |
| pronounced | nanSAWsan |

## SW89 50
## MID-WEST

| | |
|---|---|
| size | 0.6ha/1.5a |
| soil | Lime-free |
| altitude | 35m |
| rainfall | 102–114cm/40–45in |
| temperature | Zone D |
| | Plant sales |

Originally the curate's house at Ladock, occupied by the Revd Stamford Raffles Flint, the great-nephew of Sir Thomas Stamford Raffles, who established the settlement at Singapore, and grandson of Maj.-Gen. William Mudge, who carried out the first Ordnance Survey of Britain. As he became elevated from curate to rector, to a Canon, and finally to Archdeacon, so he enlarged his house and grounds. His daughter Alison married George Johnstone of **Trewithen** (56), who became his executor. The present house consists of the main entrance and west wing, with a substantial part of the original garden. From the terrace there is a view over a wide lawn to the countryside beyond. A small conservatory houses tender plants, including two lapagerias – one rose, the other white. There is a mixed border below the terrace, and the perimeter of the lawn is well furnished with shrubs and trees, with a *Cercis siliquastrum*, the Judas Tree, near the terrace.

The principal interest and attraction lies in the secret gardens in the shrubberies to the west of the lawn. At the far end, trellis work surrounds a small pond, from which paths thread through plantations of rhododendrons and camellias, for this is essentially a spring garden. Beyond is a narrow lawn with a summerhouse at one end and a greenhouse at the other, in which a plumbago and ipomoea are growing. What distinguishes this garden is the number of identified old Cornish hybrids, bred by Samuel Smith at **Penjerrick** (45), and the Gills at Tremough (see p.10). Michael Cole is also pursuing his interest in the beautiful, but now neglected Ghent azaleas. A visit to this garden will repay those interested in these classic plants, while the mass of colour will attract the non-specialist.

## 44 Nansawsan House

| | |
|---|---|
| open | Mar–Sep, Wed–Fri, Sun, pm, or by appointment |
| directions | SW77 30, 3ml SW of Falmouth between Budock and Mawnan Smith, opposite Penmorvah Manor Hotel |
| owner | Mrs Rachel Morin |
| address | Odd Acre, Penpol, Devoran, Truro TR3 6NW |
| enquiries | T:  01872 870105 |
| pronounced | penJERRick |

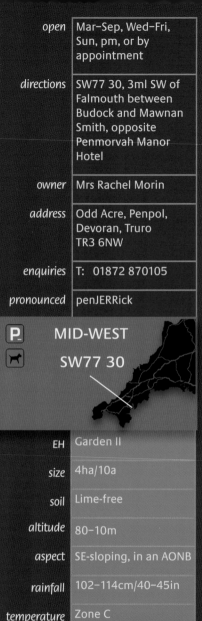

**MID-WEST**

**SW77 30**

| | |
|---|---|
| EH | Garden II |
| size | 4ha/10a |
| soil | Lime-free |
| altitude | 80–10m |
| aspect | SE-sloping, in an AONB |
| rainfall | 102–114cm/40–45in |
| temperature | Zone C |

The earliest and archetypal Cornish valley garden – a genre often dismissed as without conscious (or evident) design. Early records show this to be far from true. Robert Were Fox of **Rosehill** (37) farmed there for several years, and the estate came into his possession in 1839, when he handed over its management to his son Barclay, who began to lay out the grounds, digging pools, planting, and extending the house to become a family retreat. Barclay died in 1855, his father outliving him by 22 years. Hehad already begun experiments with exotic plants at Rosehill, and took this enthusiasm to Penjerrick on his retirement in 1872. A writer in the *Gardeners' Chronicle* of 1874 emphasized that the beauty of Penjerrick at that time depended on more than nature:

> The spot is naturally lovely, but not exceptionally so ... but I doubt if there is [anywhere] which can compete with Penjerrick in a certain indescribable effect – the effect of landscape gardening carried out with the most exquisitely cultivated taste.

After R.W. Fox's death in 1877, his only surviving daughter, Anna Maria, continued to reside there and develop the garden until her death in 1897. The head gardener, Samuel Smith, who had been appointed in 1889, was responsible for most of the plantings of rhododendrons, and proved an expert hybridizer. The old house – 'too small to be designated a mansion and far too romantic to be called a villa' – was replaced by the present dwelling in 1935. In 1987 Penjerrick was left by Janet Fox to the National Trust, who turned it down. The present owner prefers the garden jungle-like, so gumboots are recommended footwear. Penjerrick was featured on Channel Four in 2001.

## 45 Penjerrick Garden

| | |
|---|---|
| open | All year round for charity, by appointment |
| directions | SW82 38, A39 from Truro, turn on to B3289 at Playing Place to first crossroads, straight on 0.5ml short of Feock village |
| owner | Mrs Hilda Davey |
| address | Polgwynne, Feock, Truro TR3 6SG |
| enquiries | |
| | T:  01872 862612 |
| pronounced | polGWIN |

## MID-WEST
### SW82 38

| | |
|---|---|
| size | 1.8ha/4.5a |
| soil | Lime-free |
| altitude | 30m–sea |
| aspect | SE-sloping, in an AONB |
| rainfall | 102–114cm/40–45in |
| temperature | Zone C |
| | Plant sales |

Built to the east of Porthgwidden in one of the walled gardens between 1923 and 1930, when Mr and Mrs H.K. Neale were owners. At that time it occupied about six acres (2.4ha). The present grounds, developed since 1966, are smaller, but they include part of the plantation from Porthgwidden down to the sea, which was added as a protection against further development. The garden falls away in three terraces. The first, of stone, is in front of the house, from which there are views across the lawns to the estuary beyond. The second terrace is a large rectangular lawn. On the west is a bed of shrubs, beyond which, through a doorway, is entered a small formal walled garden with a rectangular pond. Beyond this is a much larger walled garden, now grassed over, in which are the greenhouses whose mechanisms were described by Canon Phillpotts in the *Journal* of the RHS in 1852. Across the lawn of the third terrace a rill runs into the foliage below, where, in the south-east corner there is a summerhouse. The whole garden is beautifully designed and richly planted. It includes what is believed to be the largest female *Gingko biloba* in Britain.

| | |
|---|---|
| open | Daily, am, pm, admission free |
| directions | SW80 31, west end of Cliff Road |
| owner | Carrick District Council |
| location | Gyllyngvase Beach, Seafront, Cliff Road, Falmouth |
| enquiries | T: 01872 224376<br>F: 01872 272239<br>smiles@carrick.gov.uk<br>www.carrick.gov.uk |

SW80 31
MID-WEST

| | |
|---|---|
| size | Small |
| soil | Neutral |
| altitude | Shore level |
| aspect | In an AONB |
| rainfall | 102–114cm/40–45in |
| temperature | Zone C |

Named after the wife of George V, the 'Queen Mary Gardens, opposite the bathing beach,' so a *Directory* states, 'were opened to the public in 1913, and were the gift of the Earl of Kimberley, the cost of laying them out being borne by the Hon. Mrs. C.S. Goldman [wife of the MP]; in front is a new promenade.' The Earl had already (in 1877) presented the town with the **Kimberley Park** (40), which was named after him. In 1903 the Council had purchased the **Gyllyngdune** estate (39), which until then occupied the land right down to the beach. This provided the opportunity to extend the road, thus creating a promenade the whole length of the cliff, up to and beyond the Falmouth Hotel. The laying out of the Queen Mary Gardens formed a part of the development of Gyllyngvase into the principal 'bathing' beach of the resort. Since then the Gardens have regularly been the scene of colourful bedding schemes, and the planting of exotics, such as agaves, aloes and puyas.

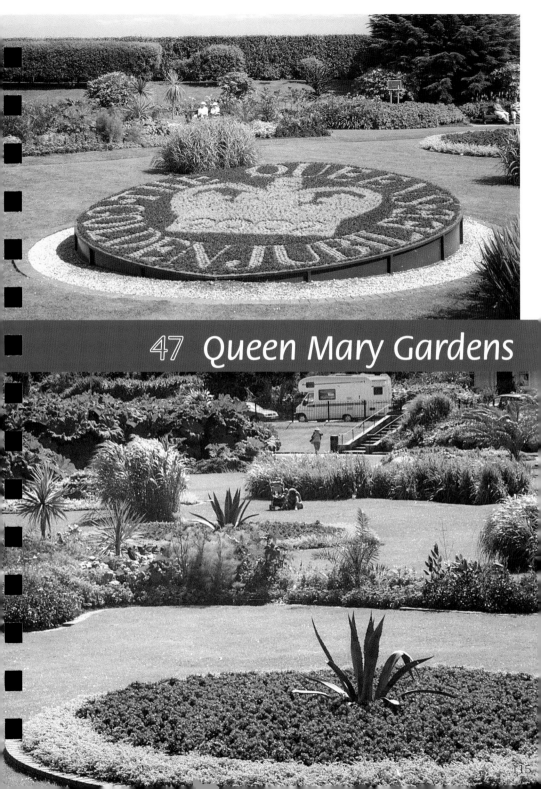

## 47 Queen Mary Gardens

| | |
|---|---|
| open | Daily |
| directions | SW84 35, turning off A3078 2ml before St Mawes |
| address | The Vicar, 16 Waterloo Close, St Mawes, Truro TR2 5BD |
| enquiries | 01326 270248 |

## MID-WEST
### SW84 35

| | |
|---|---|
| size | Medium-sized churchyard + memorial garden |
| soil | Lime-free |
| altitude | 30m to sea |
| aspect | Steeply N-sloping, in an AONB |
| rainfall | 89–102cm/35–40in |
| temperature | Zone C |

Described by Gilbert in his *Historical Survey* (1822) as being in a 'sequestered nook', and 'a valuable subject for the pencil of the artist, and admirers of landscape scenery.' In 1859 Murray's *Guide* advised that it was 'worth visiting', and many thousands have done so ever since. It seems probable that Edward Rodd, who was rector from 1803 to 1836, brought with him the horticultural expertise of his family at **Trebartha** (108) in North Hill – which he inherited in 1836 – and originated the plantings in the churchyard, which were considerably enhanced later in the century, when John Garland Treseder returned from Australia and founded a nursery alongside. Among the embellishments were a series of granite stones inscribed with verses and epigrams, lining the path down to the church, placed there by the Revd Humphrey Davis, rector from 1901 to 1930. In 1984 the Manpower Services Commission set up a project to enlarge the churchyard to designs by Neil, the grandson of J.G. Treseder, to include a pool fed by a rill. As a result of a legacy from Mrs Anne Groves, it became possible at the same time to lay out the opposite side of the road to the churchyard as Memorial Gardens, which have opened up new and higher vistas to the Creek.

48  St Just-in-Roseland
Churchyard

| | |
|---|---|
| open | Various Suns in May, Jun, Jul, pm |
| directions | SW79 48, turn off B3284 by Nature Reserve at Allet; farm is on R |
| owner | Mrs J.M. Cook |
| address | Springfield Farm, Allet, Truro TR4 9DJ |
| | T: 01872 540492 |

## MID-WEST

### SW79 48

| | |
|---|---|
| size | 1ha/2.5a |
| soil | Neutral |
| altitude | 85m |
| rainfall | 89–102cm/35–40in |
| temperature | Zone D |
| | Plant sales |

The garden at Springfield Farm arose entirely as a result of the owner's enthusiasm for horticulture, which led to her planting up this former meadow chiefly for her own interest. It is therefore of an informal design, laid out in sweeping island beds suited to contain the chosen shrubs and herbaceous specimens selected by a plantswoman. Towards the lower end of the garden, on the right, a marshy area with a natural pond, now crossed by a bridge, presented an opportunity for the creation of a bog and water garden. The pond contains mainly water lilies and aponogetum, and has been edged with herbaceous plants and shrubs. Nearby is an area of woodland where magnolias, camellias and rhododendrons have been introduced, underplanted with daffodils and erythroniums. This garden was begun in 1980 and is now reaching its maturity.

# 49 Springfield Farm

## MID-WEST

### SW80 53

| | |
|---|---|
| size | 0.8ha/2a |
| soil | Neutral to acid |
| altitude | 92m |
| rainfall | 89–102cm/35–40in |
| temperature | Zone D |
| | Plant sales |

The garden, which is in the south-west corner of a large field, was begun in 1994, following the Craigs' move from the Isle of Wight in 1972. The house, which is towards the west side of the garden, faces south, with a sun-room projecting on to a terrace lined with pot plants, one containing a splendid display of isoplexis. Among the climbers on the wall are roses, a *Clematis armandii*, jasmine, two forms of passion flower, and the climbing *Hydrangea seemannii*. Running out in line with the sun-room is a substantial pergola, with climbing roses and clematis, including the beautiful *C. florida* 'Sieboldii'; a wisteria; a fremontodendron, and other plants needing support. The boundaries of the garden are planted with conifers of various hues, backed by hedging trees, in front of which are an *Acca sellowiana* and other interesting trees and shrubs spaced as lawn specimens. Around the sides of the garden are large herbaceous borders, two of which, to the right of the pergola, form two facing arcs of a circle, the one planted with alstroemeria, the other with dahlias. To the rear of the house, the area is divided in two by a trellis with roses; the smaller part, to the east, is planted with specimen trees and bedding; to the west is partly fruit orchard, with the remainder devoted to vegetables. Along this west boundary, a stream extends the whole length of the field, down which is a long chain of semi-circular mixed shrub and herbaceous beds, each with various plantings – one, for instance, with cordylines, phormiums and other exotic plants. The field itself is mown and planted with several specimen trees and clumps. This garden has a vast range of plants to interest the plantsman, in a most attractive setting.

50 Talisonny House

| | |
|---|---|
| open | Daily all year, am, pm; entry free to RHS members |
| directions | SW76 27, follow signs from Hillhead roundabout on A39 approaching Falmouth, or Treliever Cross roundabout on junction on A39/A394 |
| owner | Trebah Garden Trust |
| address | Trebah, Mawnan Smith, Falmouth TR11 5JZ |
| enquiries | T: 01326 250448 F: 01326 250781 mail@ trebah-garden.co.uk www.trebah-garden .co.uk |
| pronounced | TREBBA, usually anglicized to TREEbaa |

MID-WEST
SW76 27

| | |
|---|---|
| EH | Garden: II |
| size | 10.5ha/26a |
| soil | Lime-free |
| altitude | 65m to estuary |
| aspect | S-sloping valley, in an AONB |
| rainfall | 102–114cm/40–45in |
| temperature | Zone C |
| | Plant centre |

The present house was built for the Nicholls family in about 1750, and was later acquired by Charles Fox, youngest brother of the **Penjerrick** (45) and **Glendurgan** (38) Foxes. Within a shelterbelt of *Pinus pinaster* and *P. radiata*, around the rim of the 26-acre valley running down to the Helford River, Charles Fox planted an arboretum as a pleasure garden. The estate was inherited by Fox's daughter Juliet and her husband Edmund Backhouse, MP, and after Charles Fox's death in 1876, the Backhouse family introduced the exotic collections of Mediterranean and sub-tropical flora for which Trebah has become famous. The garden was further developed by Charles and Alice Hext, who bought Trebah in 1907, and created the present Mallard Pond, which became home to a flock of pink flamingoes. By the mid-20th century, Bishop Hunkin was of the opinion that it was under the Hexts that the garden 'certainly reached its height'. As in the other Fox gardens, the hybridizing of rhododendrons flourished, producing the lovely 'Trebah Glory' and 'Trebah Gem'. After the death of Alice Hext in 1939, the estate was sold off in small parcels, and for the next 42 years the house and garden fell into decay. Trebah was bought by the Hibbert family in 1981, and they began a long programme of restoration and development. They opened the garden to the public in 1987, and three years later created the Trebah Garden Trust, donating to it the house, garden and cottages. In recent years, Trebah has received grants from the Heritage Lottery Fund and Objective One for a new visitor centre and garden enhancement. It is now one of the leading attractions in Cornwall, and the garden has been secured for the enjoyment of the public for all time.

| | |
|---|---|
| open | One Sun in Apr, pm, and during village festival in Jun |
| directions | SW91 39, adjoining Trist House |
| owners | Dr & Mrs A.G. Cowen |
| address | Tregarthen, Veryan, Truro TR2 5QA |
| enquiries | T: 01872 501542 |
| pronounced | treGARTHen |

## MID-WEST

### SW91 39

| | |
|---|---|
| size | c.0.4ha/1a |
| soil | Lime-free |
| altitude | 75m |
| aspect | In an AONB |
| rainfall | 89–102cm/35–40in |
| temperature | Zone C |

A contemporary bungalow, Tregarthen is reached at the top of the drive alongside the Village Stores/Post Office. It can also be entered from **Trist House** (57) when it is opened at the same time. The path runs from the remarkable rockery, entering the wild part of Tregarthen through a gate and thence, via a bridge over the stream with many water plants, to the main lawn, and a terrace at the rear of the house, overhung with wisteria. The main garden rises up steps from the lawn, which is planted in mixed shrub and flower borders overtopped with trees. From this area, above the side of the house, runs a long pergola covered with roses and wisteria, which opens into three compartments, one with vegetables, another with a sundial. The path then sweeps down to the front of the house, where, among other trees are mature magnolias, including the fine *Magnolia* 'Star Wars'. The garden has been developing since 1994, and was opened for the first time in 2000.

52 Tregarthen

| | |
|---|---|
| open | Daily, mid-Feb–end Oct, am, pm; Sun pm; tel for winter opening |
| directions | SW83 39, off A39 Truro–Falmouth road at Playing Place, on B3289 to King Harry Ferry; just before ferry |
| owner | NT |
| address | Trelissick, Feock, Truro TR3 6QL |
| enquiries | T: 01872 862090 F: 01872 865808 trelissick@national trust.org.uk www. nationaltrust.org.uk |
| pronounced | treLISsick |
| EH | House: II*; water-tower, kitchen garden walls, etc, II |

MID-WEST
SW83 39

| | |
|---|---|
| EH | Garden: II* |
| size | 8ha/20a + 152ha/376a parkland |
| soil | Shillet on clay, lime-free |
| altitude | 50m to river |
| aspect | E-sloping, in an AONB |
| rainfall | 102–114cm/40–45in |
| temperature | Zone C |
| NC | Photinias and Azaras |
| | Plant centre |

Descriptions of Trelissick have focused on the parkland, which is of a kind unusual in Cornwall. The first modern house was built in about 1750 to designs by Edmund Davy, grandfather of the celebrated Humphry Davy. The estate was bought in 1790 by the wealthy mine-owner 'guinea-a-minute' Daniell, whose son, Thomas, engaged Peter Frederick Robinson in 1824 to rebuild the house, described by Pevsner as 'the severest neo-Greek mansion in Corn-wall'. He laid out extensive rides through the beautiful hanging woods along the west side of the estuary, and planted particularly beech and deciduous oaks in the park. However, his extravagant style of life eventually obliged him to sell his estate. By 1854 it had passed to Carew Davies Gilbert, who raised a sec-ond storey on the wings of the house; introduced 'a fair sprinkling of foreign trees and shrubs from his wander-ings into remote regions of the globe', and began laying out the Carcaddon area, over the bridge, as a garden. In the 1930s the estate was still largely shrubberies beneath a canopy of oak and beech, with some fine conifers.

The present garden is the creation of Mrs Ida Copeland and her husband Ronald, a director of Spode – many of the flowers painted on their porcelain being grown at Trelis-sick. Together they planted the garden and the Dell with trees and shrubs, including hybrid rhododen-drons from Bodnant, from 1928 onwards. In 1955 Mrs Copeland donated the property to the National Trust, who opened up the vista to **Tregothnan** (120). Among the many features, the log summerhouse, and the water-tower with its squirrel weather-vane, from the crest of the Gilbert family, are noteworthy.

53 Trelissick

| | |
|---|---|
| open | One Sun Aug, pm, or by appointment |
| directions | SW75 28, on Truro to Helston/Falmouth road, A39/A394. Follow signs for Constantine, at High Cross garage, 1.5ml before Constantine, turn L signed Mawnan, R after 30yd down dead-end lane: 0.5ml at end of lane |
| owner | Mrs L.M. Nottingham |
| address | Trenarth, Constantine TR11 5JN |
| enquiries | T:  01326 340444 |
| pronounced | treNARTH |

P ⛾

MID-WEST

SW75 28

| | |
|---|---|
| size | 0.8ha/3a |
| soil | Lime-free |
| altitude | From 50m |
| aspect | SE-sloping, in an AONB |
| rainfall | 102–114cm/40–45in |
| temperature | Zone C |

The grounds are entered by way of a wide approach that opens on to a view of the countryside beyond, where the woods run down to the Helford river. The drive then turns by a terraced area to reveal the house below. This old farmhouse, which has a date-stone for 1748 on one gable, has been much enlarged and modernized over the centuries. Upon descending, the mildness of the climate is at once evidenced by the sight of a range of tender shrubs, including a large *Daphne bholua* and a variety of cannas and hedychiums. To the rear, an arch leads into an attractive Elizabethan courtyard, which has the date 1658 and the arms of Trenarth and Trefusis with the motto 'GOD GIVETH STRENGTH' on a lead plaque over the doorway. The main ornamental garden lies on the slopes above the house, which is sheltered on three sides by a long, 18th-century wall, which has been listed by English Heritage. It has been made a feature on the outside by the planting of a long row of hydrangeas and Japanese anemones for late summer and autumn interest. Within this wall, the more recent planting is formal, within several yew 'rooms' containing vegetables, flower borders and a pergola. One of these leads to a handsome wrought-iron commemorative gate. Trenarth exhibits a charming association of modern planting in an ancient setting.

54 Trenarth

| | |
|---|---|
| open | Several Suns Feb, Mar, Apr, pm |
| directions | SW84 50, from Truro take A39 Newquay road through St Erme, turn R to Trevella at end of Trispen |
| owners | The Hon. Mrs D. Verney & Ms R. Verney |
| address | Trevella, St Erme, Truro TR4 9BD |
| enquiries | T: 01872 510361 or 510504 rosie@fsnet.co.uk |
| pronounced | treVELLa |

**MID-WEST**

**SW84 50**

| | |
|---|---|
| size | 1.6ha/4a |
| soil | Lime-free |
| altitude | 90m |
| rainfall | 102–114cm/40–45in |
| temperature | Zone D |

The house at Trevella is early 19th century, adjoining a farm, and curiously orientated so that the main door is rarely used, in favour of a back entrance through a conservatory. The side of the house faces the lawn and ha-ha, edged with belts of trees and rhododendrons. The main drive rises through lines of cherry trees before arriving at thin woodland near the house, similar to that leading out to the farm on the other side. Both are carpeted in the spring by a succession of snowdrops, primroses and bluebells, and other wild flowers, such as fritillaries, the open days being synchronized with their corresponding seasons. The high rhododendron and camellia hedges stem from plants brought by Mrs Verney upon moving from **Tregothnan** (120) in 1954, and the whole garden has been made since that date. The conservatory leads out on to the walled garden fringed with mixed borders, lush in springtime with various hostas, hellebores and euphorbias. By a parrotia – one of the few trees to have autumn colouring in Cornwall – the ornamental garden passes into a further section grassed over, but with an impressive line of five mature espalier apple trees. A door to the right leads out into another lightly wooded area, which is being developed as a 'Millenium Garden' with camellias, shrub roses, tree ferns, and rhododendrons – some of the 'grande' series.

## 55 *Trevella*

Mar–Sep, Mon–Sat, +
Sun Apr, May, am, pm;
walled garden: Jun,
Mon, Tues. Free to RHS
members Jul–Sep

SW91 47, 0.5ml E
of Probus; on A390
Truro–St Austell road

Mr A.M.J. Galsworthy

Grampound Road,
Truro TR2 4DD

T:  01726 883647
F:  01726 882301
gardens@trewithen
estate.demon.co.uk
www.trewithen
gardens.co.uk

treWITHen

House, 2 pavilions:
each I; barn, 2 engine
houses II*

D-WEST

N91 47

Garden: II*

10ha/25a

Lime-free

85–80m

S-facing

102–114cm/40–45in

Zone C

Nursery: wide-ranging,
specializing in tender
species

After a checkered family history, the old house at Trewithen, which had been enlarged for Thomas Hawkins by Thomas Edwards of Greenwich, was altered for Philip Hawkins in 1763–4 to designs by Sir Robert Taylor; but it was Thomas who was principally responsible for the major planting. The Record Office contains a notebook on 'The Care and Cultivation of Trees', written by him in 1745, and a 'Diary' written in 1757 by his father-in-law James Heywood. Woods were described to the south and south-west, which protected the house from the prevailing winds, and avenues radiating to the east and north. Thomas died in 1766, to be succeeded by his son, later Sir Christopher Hawkins, who was more interested in enlarging his estate than improving his grounds.

The 'Golden Age' began early in the 20th century after the succession of George Horace Johnstone in 1904, who first planted 100 hybrids of *Rhododendron arboreum*, two of which were named 'Alison Johnstone', after his wife, and 'Jack Skilton', after his gardener. Compulsory wartime tree-felling provided an opportunity to reshape and plant the lawn, which is now one of the outstanding features of the garden. Trewithen is renowned for its

unique collection of tender and rare plants. Among them are *Camellias*, such as their own 'Elizabeth Johnstone' and 'Glenn's Orbit', and 'Donation', struck from the original at Borde Hill. G.H. Johnstone was also celebrated for his raising of daffodils, and his collection of magnolias, on which he was an authority. Among the garden features are the walled garden with its lily pond and summerhouse, and the Cock Pit, a former quarry and now a rock garden. More recently platforms have been constructed for viewing this exceptional garden.

56 Trewithen

| | |
|---|---|
| open | Apr–Sep, Sun, Tue, pm, other times by arrangement |
| directions | SW91 39, from centre of Veryan on Portloe road, just past PO |
| owners | Mr & Mrs Graham Salmon |
| address | Trist House, Veryan, Truro TR2 5QA |
| enquiries | T:  01872 501422<br>F:  01872 501211<br>graham@<br>tristobs.ndo.co.uk |
| EH | House: II; lodge II |

MID-WEST

SW91 39

| | |
|---|---|
| size | 2ha/5a |
| soil | Lime-free |
| altitude | 80–65m |
| aspect | NW-sloping, in an AONB |
| rainfall | 89–102cm/35–40in |
| temperature | Zone C |
| | Plant sales |

After the death of his father, Samuel Trist exchanged his Devon living with his successor, to become the third in the family to be instituted as vicar of Veryan. Since his mother continued to live in his father's mansion at Behan Park, he took over the vicarage from his brother Thomas, and in 1831 engaged Harrison, a London architect, to rebuild it, with a new lodge incorporating ornamental masonry from St Nun's Chapel in Grampound. He then commenced to lay out an elaborate garden at a cost of £1,000, which, in comparison with the £3,000 spent on the house, was a vast sum. The present owners, however, found the garden overgrown and in a somewhat dilapidated state, although gradually they have been able to discover what still remains of the original. There is a Victorian rose arch and a Folly above the house, and in front three terraces ornamented with vases, with a central pillar, which leads down to the lawn. Their most astonishing discovery, however, lies to the west of the drive, where removal of undergrowth revealed an extensive rockery, with a pool, and possibly the remains of a grotto, which bears a striking resemblance to similar rockwork at Hoole House, Chester, illustrated in the *Villa Gardener* of 1838. The remainder of the garden has been greatly developed since 1994 by the addition of mixed planting on the lawn below the terraces, alongside which has been constructed a substantial pergola leading up to further bedding and plantations above. With the restoration of original features, and especially of the spectacular rockwork, this has established Trist House as the most important surviving parsonage garden in Cornwall.

| | |
|---|---|
| open | Daily, am, pm, entrance free |
| directions | SW82 45, entrance from St George's Road or by Crown Court |
| owner | Truro City Council |
| location | Edward Street, Truro |
| | T: 01872 274766<br>F: 01872 225572 |

MID-WEST

SW82 45

| | |
|---|---|
| size | Waterfall Gardens: 0.3ha/0.75a; Victoria Park: c.1.6ha/4a |
| soil | Lime-free |
| aspect | Steeply W-sloping |
| rainfall | 102–114cm/40–45in |
| temperature | Zone C |

During the development of Truro towards the end of the 19th century, the remaining freeholds of Lord Falmouth in the city were auctioned off in 1891, affording an opportunity for the purchase of a plot of land leading to the Tregear waterfall, near St George's Methodist Church, which was presented to the City in 1893. This was described as 'prettily laid out [by John Mitchinson, the Truro nursery-man] with flower beds, shrubs &c., and skirted by the Kenwyn stream, which [created] an ornamental waterfall', from which the garden derived its name. Subsequently, new legislation made it possible for the Council to provide pleasure gardens at pub-lic expense, and this resulted in the laying out of Victoria Park on the steep slopes above, between the Waterfall Gardens and Castle Hill, now the site of the Crown Court. This was opened, as a tablet records, in 1898 in commemoration of the 60th year of the reign of Queen Victoria. There were also at that time an ornamental fountain, a bandstand, a drinking fountain presented in commemoration of the Queen's 81st birthday, an aquar-ium, and a caretaker's lodge in com-memoration of the coronation of King Edward VII. If the gardens are entered through the little gate and alleyway just below the Crown Court, the view opens on to a brilliant display of colourful bedding, leading down to the Victorian bandstand. The Parks' Department, which enters the 'Britain in Bloom' com-petition, have regularly received awards for their planting in this and other areas of the City. The railway viaduct towers over both gardens, offering a view of the Park that is a charming introduction to the city for the traveller entering the station from the east.

## 58 Victoria Park & Waterfall Gardens

## Grampound and Mevagissey

Grampound owed its initial success to its 'Great Bridge' (in Norman French *grand-pont*), which has been there since at least 1296, and was so-called because it was the main medieval highway crossing the then much broader River Fal, along the way from Truro to St Austell. Of three tanneries in the town in the 19th century, only one survived until recently, belonging to the Croggon family, whose houses, **The Hollies** (66) and **Creed** (62), have fine contemporary gardens. The quaintness of Mevagissey has long appealed to tourists, who are now additionally attracted to the no longer 'lost' gardens of **Heligan** (71), cultivated by the Tremayne family for some 300 years, and now themselves overshadowed by **The Eden Project** (63). But neither should detract from the colourful history of **Caerhays** (61) under the Trevanions (relatives of Lord Byron), or its present horticultural distinction.

*(See gardens 61, 62, 66, 84.)*

## St Austell, Lostwithiel and Fowey

St Austell owed its origin and increasing prosperity to mining – in two forms. Its early growth depended upon tin, particularly from the rich mine at Carclaze, which operated continuously from the 16th century until 1851; but though relatively ancient, the town never received a charter. Its greatest prosperity came in the late 18th century, as a result of experiments by the Wedgwoods to increase the strength and quality of their porcelain. From this time, St Austell was the centre of the china clay industry, allowing families like the Rashleighs of Fowey to create their country estates. Charles Rashleigh built the harbour at Charlestown to export clay, and landscaped **Menacuddle** (74), Prideaux House, and Duporth. However, **Tregrehan** (85), former seat of the Bodrugans, predates the town, and is opposite **Pine Lodge** (78) – probably our finest contemporary garden.

Lostwithiel is much older than St Austell, flourishing first as a ford at the high-water mark of the Fowey estuary; then under the protection of the royal dukes at Restormel Castle, and finally as the principal Stannary town, with the Court and 'Duchy Palace'. Eventually, it lost its place as a port to Fowey, whose natural harbour was the most important south-coast port in the 14th century. However, its steep valley sides precluded Fowey from expanding. **Headland** (64), at the mouth of the estuary, has been developed as a remarkable cliff garden, while **Boconnoc** (59), near Lostwithiel, is among the greatest ancient Cornish estates.

*(See gardens 59, 63, 64, 65, 71, 73, 74, 78, 80, 82, 85.)*

## Newquay, Padstow and Wadebridge

Newquay, Padstow and Wadebridge, the three focal points in the north, although of differing origins, share a common history as fishing ports. This was always the function of Newquay. Padstow grew up around the monastery of St Petroc.

Grampound
Mevagissey
St Austell
Lostwithiel
Fowey
Newquay
Padstow
Wadebridge
Bodmin

# 4 MID-EAST

Its wide, sandy estuary was ideal for the seine fishing of pilchards, which provided secular employment and prosperity. The origin and history of Wadebridge is encapsulated in its name – 'Wade', an early medieval low-tide crossing of the Camel.

Newquay boasted no great houses until the Regency craving for the sea air led a few wealthy landowners to set up marine residences. But **Trenance Gardens** (86) are a fine example of a public park. However, there are ancient and great houses in the vicinity, especially **Trerice** (87), and **Tresillian House** (88). Central to Padstow is **Prideaux Place** (81), dominating the town. Yet exposure of the north coast to the elements has been a deterrent to the creation of large gardens, and only one – **Long Cross** (70) – is in the gazetteer.

*(See gardens 67, 70, 81, 86, 87, 88.)*

## Bodmin

Bodmin is the only town in Cornwall mentioned in the 'Domesday Book', where it was recorded that the Canons of St Petroc owned 68 houses and a market, making it probably the most populous place in the county. When it received its charter in the 13th century, the strong religious life around the monastery sustained the markets and fairs that brought great wealth. After a relative decline in the 17th and 18th centuries, Bodmin re-emerged in the 19th century as a route centre. Its eventual loss of status may have been due in part to a refusal to allow the railway into the town. In 1988 the transfer of the Law Courts to Truro, which already held the County Hall and Cathedral, spelt the end for Bodmin as the County Town. Over the centuries, Cornwall's centre of gravity moved from Launceston, to Bodmin, and finally to Truro, which is truly central. A number of important historic gardens are grouped around Bodmin, including that of the Robartes family at **Lanhydrock** (69), and of Sir William Molesworth at **Pencarrow** (77).

*(See gardens 60, 68, 69, 72, 75, 76, 77, 79, 83.)*

| | |
|---|---|
| open | One Sun May, pm, and all year for groups of 15+ by appointment |
| directions | SX14 60, on A390 enter by Middle Taphouse, follow signs |
| owners | Mr & Mrs A. Fortescue |
| address | Boconnoc, Lostwithiel PL22 0RG |
| enquiries | T: 01208 872507 F: 01208 873836 adgfortescue@ btinternet.com |
| pronounced | boCONock |
| EH | House: II*; dovecote; bathing pool, bath-house, obelisk, 2 classical shrines, 4 lodges: each II |

## MID-EAST
### SX14 60

| | |
|---|---|
| EH | Garden + deer park: II* |
| size | Ornamental gardens in extensive grounds |
| soil | Lime-free |
| aspect | Sloping variously, 140–40m; house at 60m, in a SAGLV |
| rainfall | 102–114cm/40–45in |
| temperature | Zone E |
| | Plant stall |

The Domesday manor of Boconnoc has a long and distinguished history, with the deer park – licensed in 1381 – being the only medieval park in Cornwall to have survived to the present day. The estate was purchased in 1717 by Thomas Pitt, Governor of Madras, from the proceeds of his sale of the 'Pitt Diamond'. His grandson, William 1st Earl of Chatham, was a patron of 'Capability Brown' and an amateur landscaper, who may have influenced his brother Thomas in 'improving' his estate. Thomas's son, the 2nd Baron Camelford, was an exponent of the 'picturesque' style, and added his contribution to the landscape, so that Gilbert, in his *Historical Survey* (1822), wrote that 'the pleasing scenery of nature is viewed in all its different attitudes, whilst the decorations of art are lost to the eye, and almost to the imagination'. William Mason, the celebrated poet of the *English Garden* (1772), is reported to have remarked that the River Lerryn flowing through Boconnoc 'was a much handsomer nymph than his Nottinghamshire Ligea, and had he been earlier acquainted with her charms, should certainly have occupied her place in his poem'. During the 19th century, a Pinetum was added, and various plantings of beech and conifers were made. The house, now being restored, rests upon a platform below the rock face on which the church stands. There are ornamental gardens on this level, with a fountain, pond, dovecote, and bath-house. However, the greatest beauty of Boconnoc lies in its landscape – the wooded slopes; the lake now restored; the valley of the Lerryn, and the long drive passing the obelisk erected in 1771, framed by two classical shrines. This is an historic site, where Charles I made his headquarters during the Civil War.

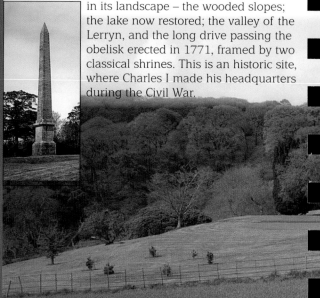

# 59 Boconnoc

| | |
|---|---|
| open | Suns mid May–first in Jul, pm, and by appointment |
| directions | SX03 65, turn at Bodmin Trailer Centre (A30) signposted Nanstallon, L at crossroads signposted Hoopers Bridge, then sharp R |
| owner | Martin Appleton |
| address | Bodwannack Manor, Nanstallon, Bodmin PL30 5LN |
| enquiries | T: 01208 831427 |
| pronounced | bodWANnack |

## MID-EAST

### SX03 65

| | |
|---|---|
| size | 0.6ha/1.5a |
| soil | Lime-free |
| altitude | 60m |
| rainfall | 114–127cm/45–50in |
| temperature | Zone E |

A manor dating from the 12th century, the present old and romantic house with a slate-floored verandah and rough-hewn granite pillars was built on the original site, with the 'Bodwannack Cross' in the centre of the front lawn. To the left of the entrance drive is the vegetable garden, below which is a wide grass pathway with large rhododendrons on the left, and a rose bed on the right. Above this bed is a long pergola covered with a white wisteria, forming the lower boundary of the vegetable garden. Along another side are three rose arches. The pathway leads out into a grassed area where a stone circle has been set up using boulders from an ancient mine. Upon returning along the upper side of the kitchen garden, the path down to the house passes between rockwork planted with hostas and other herbaceous plants. The house and its garden is separate, on the right of the approach, entered between two small beds of dwarf conifers. There is a conservatory with an array of streptocarpus, and a wall supporting several pots of begonias, flanked by an orange and lemon tree. The garden is richly planted, especially on the rising ground above a pond, fringed with acers, astilbe, ornamental grasses and a conifer. A collection of some 50 daffodils contrasts with the rhododendrons and camellias in the springtime. This is a varied and interesting garden with an aura of antiquity.

60  Bodwannack Manor

| | |
|---|---|
| open | Garden: Mar–Jun, daily am, pm; house: mid-Mar–first week May, Mon–Fri, incl bank holidays, pm. Free to RHS members in Mar |
| directions | SW97 41, Mevagissey turn on A390 E of Grampound; signed |
| owner | Julian Williams |
| address | Estate Office, Gorran, St Austell PL26 6LY |
| enquiries | T: 01872 501310 F: 01872 501870 estateoffice@ caerhays.co.uk www.caerhays.co.uk |
| pronounced | C'RAZE |
| EH | House: I; many garden features I and II |

## MID-EAST

### SW97 41

| | |
|---|---|
| EH | Grounds: II* |
| size | 24ha/60a |
| soil | Lime-free |
| altitude | 70m–sea; house 25m |
| aspect | NE-, N-, and E-sloping, in an AONB |
| rainfall | 89–102cm/35-40in |
| temperature | Zone C |
| NC | Magnolias |
| | Plant sales |

From about 1379 Caerhays belonged to the Trevanions, later related to Lord Byron. Between 1805 and 1807 John Bettesworth Trevanion engaged the celebrated John Nash to build the present Castle. Described as a 'folly', it certainly bankrupted the Trevanions. It then lay unfinished and derelict until purchased in 1854 by Michael Williams of **Scorrier** (23), whose grandson, J.C. Williams, may be regarded as the founder of the great reputation of Caerhays as a plantsman's garden of national, perhaps international importance. He sponsored or contributed to several plant-hunting expeditions, notably those of Forrest, Wilson, Farrer and Kingdon Ward, and the gardens reflect their discoveries of rhododendrons, azaleas, camellias and magnolias. Other collections were made of hydrangeas, lithocarpus and nothofagus. Seeds from these expeditions were sent back to the contributors, and were propagated and planted in the grounds above the Castle. Many of these introduced specimens and varieties flowered for the first time at Caerhays. J.C. Williams also interested himself in breeding hybrids, of which 12 appear in the *Register* – 'Blue Tit', 'Humming Bird', 'Yellow Hammer', and 'Royal Flush' being best known. Of equal, or perhaps greater fame were the

camellia crosses made between *Camellia japonica* and *saluensis*, which have become known as *williamsii* camellias. Among these are 'J.C. Williams' and 'Mary Christian', named after J.C. and his wife, and 'Charles Michael', named after his gardener. In 1893, J.C. Williams also began to raise daffodils. In a recent survey of *Champion Trees*, 13 were recorded here, to which a further nine may be added. For these and many other reasons, Caerhays may justly be regarded as the most important plantsman's garden in Cornwall.

# 61 Caerhays Castle Gardens

| | |
|---|---|
| open | Feb–Oct, daily, am, pm |
| directions | SW93 47, from centre of Grampound on A390, take road signed to Creed. After 1ml turn L opposite Creed Church, garden on L |
| owners | Mr & Mrs William Croggon |
| address | Creed House, Creed, Grampound, Truro TR2 4SL |
| | T: 01872 530372 |

P

## MID-EAST

### SW93 47

| | |
|---|---|
| size | 2ha/5a |
| soil | Lime-free |
| altitude | 35m |
| aspect | W-sloping |
| rainfall | 102–114cm/40–45in |
| temperature | Zone D |
| | Plant sales |

Formerly the rectory of the parish of St Crida, Creed House was built around 1730, with its extensive grounds sloping west-wards. When the Croggons arrived in 1974, the garden was totally overgrown, and took them about ten years to bring back into shape enough to begin serious plant-ing. There is a range of buildings behind the house, where various forms of garden are being created. A derelict summerhouse was restored in 1977. The stables have two cobbled areas in front, the lower of which is concave, and was probably intended as a carriage-wash. To the rear, the walled garden, at first used for vegetables, has been lawned, and contrasting herbaceous borders are being developed. Rising from this lawn are steps to the top woodland of some 2.5 acres (1ha) planted with indigenous trees. The west front of the house, with borders and a terrace, looks down on to a large, flat lawn, probably originally intended for bowls or croquet. This drops to the naturally sloping lawn beyond, the bank planted with spring bulbs. The garden principally consists of a deep belt, presenting from the house a rich tapestry of colour and texture, through which wind many walks among planta-tions of trees with underplanting of shrubs. Here are a group of calocedrus and an acer modelled on those at Westonbirt. A large pond has a terrace whose paving is threaded with camomile and peppermint (*Mentha requienii*), which leads into a bog garden planted with skunk cabbage, cande-labra primulas, ferns and mecanopsis. The object in the planting of the walks has been not only to give variety, but to open vistas, some looking out over the surrounding countryside, others looking inwards to paths lit by broken sunlight.

62  Creed Gardens

| | |
|---|---|
| open | Daily, excl 24, 25 Dec, am, pm |
| directions | SX04 54, signed with brown signs from A30 and A390 |
| owners | The Eden Trust |
| address | The Eden Project, Bodelva, St Austell PL24 2SG |
| enquiries | T: 01726 811911 F: 01726 811912 esteel@ edenproject.com www. edenproject.com |

MID-EAST

SX04 54

| | |
|---|---|
| size | Extensive former china-clay pit, c.20ha/50a |
| soil | Composted |
| altitude | 105m |
| rainfall | 114–127cm/45–50in |
| temperature | Zone E |
| | Plant centre |

Cornwall's major tourist attraction, and the first port of call for almost every visitor to the county, the Eden Project opened in 2001. The sight of the vast 'biomes', like giant soap bubbles, is the first cause of astonishment; the second, upon entering them, is the virtuosity of the engineering that has made all this possible. The whole complex occupies a vast pit resulting from the commercial extraction of china clay – a medium in itself inhospitable to plant life, but which has been made fertile by composting. The larger biome represents the humid tropics, planted with many tropical varieties, including fully-grown trees, around a grand water feature pouring down over the cliff side. To maintain humidity, there is a regular emission of mist, which further enhances the impression of a 'rain forest'. The smaller biome represents the warm temperate, or Mediterranean zone, and its planting includes olives, grape vines, citrus fruits, agaves, and other succulents, some of which grow outdoors in Cornwall at gardens as such **Lamorran House** (42) on the mainland, and the **Abbey Gardens** (1) at Tresco. A third biome is in prospect, to represent the arid or desert zone. The surrounding grounds, which are extensive, are landscaped with large-scale designs and sculptures to suit the great size of the arena, which is also used for a variety of events and concerts. Eden is described as a 'Project', since its ultimate purpose is not so much entertainment as education. Its aim has been to replace the formality of outdated botanic gardens, by promulgating its central message – that humanity is dependent upon the plant world. For this reason, alongside the visitor attractions, shops and plant sales, there are exhibitions and talks, and ancillary study and training centres.

63 The Eden Project

| | |
|---|---|
| open | May–mid-Sep, Thu pm |
| directions | SX12 50, by ferry from Fowey + 10-min walk along West Street and up Battery Lane. By car follow signs to Polruan on E side of estuary, ignore 1st car-park, turn L and park in 2nd car-park (overlooking harbour), turn L (on foot) down St Saviour's Hill |
| owners | Jean and John Hill |
| address | Headland, Battery Lane, Polruan by Fowey PL23 1PW |
| enquiries | T: 01726 870243 |

## MID-EAST

## SX12 50

| | |
|---|---|
| size | 0.5ha/1.25a |
| soil | Neutral |
| aspect | W-sloping, 30m to sea, in an AONB |
| rainfall | 89–102cm/35–40in |
| temperature | Zone D |

Headland Garden was first laid out when the house was built between 1900 and 1915 in a quarry, when much topsoil must have been brought in before planting. The present owners bought the house in 1974, not for the garden, but as a holiday home. Yet down the years it has attracted widespread attention from the media, and was once the setting for a film. The garden is perched high on a cliff, exposed to the sea and wind on three sides. There is a successful vegetable garden at the top of a precipitous drop to a small cove below, which is accessible down steps. The walls, paths and arches, which blend with the natural slates, were constructed by John Hill and Peter Ball. Shelter, which is essential, was from the outset provided by the Monterey Pine (*Pinus radiata*), most now past their best, but with new ones growing to the same height. Hawthorn and Mountain Ash have proved successful, although distorted, and also olearia and the *Genista* 'Porlock'; lower hedges of escallonia, *Hippophae rhamnoides*, and euonymous moulded into the shape of the rock provide shelter behind them even for exotics such as agaves, aloes, aeoniums, lampranthus, the Hottentot Fig *Carprobotus edulis*, and also *Aptenia cordifolia* from Israel. Headland has been open for many years for charity, and in 2000 received an award from the RNLI for raising a total of £22,000. However, the garden has qualities that will appeal to many, whether or not they wish to support the RNLI.

# 64 Headland Garden

| | |
|---|---|
| open | Mar–Oct, daily, am, pm |
| directions | SX08 55, off A390, take B3269 signed Fowey, within 200yd fork R signed Treesmill and follow signs |
| owner | Tricia Howard |
| address | Hidden Valley, Treesmill, nr Par PL24 2TU |
| enquiries | T: 01208 873225 www.hiddenvalley gardens.co.uk |

**MID-EAST**

**SX09 56**

| | |
|---|---|
| size | Medium |
| soil | Lime-free |
| altitude | From 25m |
| aspect | S-facing |
| rainfall | 102–114cm/40–45in |
| temperature | Zone D |
| | Nursery: specializes in herbaceous and cottage plants |

The Howard family moved in 1999 from Northern Yorkshire to the very different climate of Cornwall, bringing with them over 1,000 plants, with the intention of setting up a garden and nursery on a site that had been run as a soft-fruit small-holding. The house is a convert-ed stone barn, with the entrance gravelled and formally planted with raised beds. Below the nursery is a long bed of 'hot' col-ours and purple foliage, leading down to a pool fed by a stream running through woodland, which has yet to be developed. To the side of the house are two large rectangular beds with four golden yews, which will even-tually be trimmed into cones. Around the greenhouse are stock beds, and the beginning of a Mediterranean garden with cistus, rosemary, myrtle, laven-der, and *Convolvulus sabatius*. This garden is still in its infancy, but has much to offer, and great potential.

## 65 Hidden Valley Gardens & Nurseries

| | |
|---|---|
| open | Apr–Sep by appointment only, pm |
| directions | SW93 48, on A390 in centre of village, towards the higher end |
| owner | Mrs N.B. Croggon |
| address | The Hollies, Grampound, Truro TR2 4QS |
| enquiries | T: 01726 882474 |
| EH | House: II |

## MID-EAST
## SW93 48

| | |
|---|---|
| size | 0.8ha/2a |
| soil | Lime-free |
| altitude | 50m |
| aspect | SW-sloping, in an AGLV |
| rainfall | 102–114cm/40–45in |
| temperature | Zone D |

Dating possibly from the early 18th century, with mid- to late-19th century alterations, The Hollies is a town house fronting immediately on to the single road of the ancient town of Grampound. Behind the house is a courtyard garden with outbuildings and a greenhouse, leading into another enclosed area, of lawn with perimeter borders, which itself leads into a smaller paved enclosure, appropriately bedded with alpines and other similar plants. These enclosures represent the town garden, but beyond there would originally have been a medieval 'stitch', and it is in these fields that the larger part of the garden has been created, in the form of island beds variously planted. The sequence and design add to the charm, but it is the wide range and expert plantings by Mrs Croggon that raise this garden well above the average. Across the road the leather tannery, which had long been in the Croggon family, and was one of the very few to have survived using traditional methods with oak bark, sadly is now closed.

66 The Hollies

| | |
|---|---|
| open | Daily, excl 25 Dec–1Jan, am, pm |
| directions | SW87 66, in centre of village |
| owners | Rob & Stella Hore |
| address | The Japanese Garden & Bonsai Nursery, St Mawgan, Newquay TR8 4ET |
| enquiries | T: 01637 860116 F: 01637 860887 rob@thebonsai nursery.com www.thebonsai nursery.com |

## MID-EAST

### SW87 66

| | |
|---|---|
| size | 0.6ha/1.5a |
| soil | Lime-free |
| aspect | In an AGLV |
| rainfall | 102–114cm/40–45in |
| temperature | Zone D |
| | Nursery: specializes in bonsai |

The idea for a Japanese Garden began in 1988, when Robert Hore and his wife Stella returned to his native Cornwall from London. The chosen site was a run-down smallholding, which required clearing. The inspiration came from the unexpected gift of a bonsai, which aroused an enthusiasm issuing in a determination to do something about it. The garden does not necessarily follow orthodox rules precisely, although it is the result of much study, and has won the approval of Japanese visitors. The focal point is the tea house, representing a traditional Japanese ceremony, whose balcony overlooks the beautiful Koi pond and waterfall. Another characteristic feature is the Zen garden of tranquillity, which is without plants, and consists solely of carefully placed rocks on sand brought to life daily by raking. Plants do nonetheless play an important part, especially the conifers, bamboos, camellias and acers. These bring colour and texture to the planting, the vibrant colours of the springtime azaleas contrasting with the dying hues of the acers in autumn. The garden first opened to the public in 1997, when its appearance of maturity belied the relatively short period of its creation. This was made possible by incorporating existing mature trees, and by importing well-weathered stone.

The Bonsai Nursery forms an integral part of the whole concept – indeed, the garden has grown out of the nursery, rather than, as is often the case, being merely an added extra. Japanese gardens are fashionable, although often little more than a corner of an English garden with a pond, a bridge, a lantern and an acer. A visit to this garden will induce the authentic atmosphere of the real thing.

| | |
|---|---|
| open | Two Suns Aug, pm |
| directions | SX07 67, N side of town, 100yd up hill from Westberry Hotel |
| owners | Dr & Mrs M.S. Stead |
| address | Kingberry, 38 Rhind Street, Bodmin PL31 2EL |
| enquiries | See NGS annual yellow book or www.ngs.org.uk |

**P** **MID-EAST**

**SX07 67**

| | |
|---|---|
| size | 0.4ha/1a |
| soil | Alkaline |
| rainfall | 114–127cm/45–50in |
| temperature | Zone D |
| | Plant stall |

The narrow entrance from the street belies the extent and richness of the garden beyond. The old house was built in 1830, facing south at a right angle to the road. When the present owners arrived in 1991, the grounds were principally given over to market gardening and fruit. The walls of the house at the entrance are still covered with a 100-year-old pear tree bearing tiny, though sweet fruit. The garden to the front is lawned, with wide herbaceous borders of mixed colours, influenced by combinations seen at Bosvigo (34). The far side of the house is mostly taken up by a fine conservatory, with two puyas in pots by the door, which looks out over a long lawn with a serpentine herbaceous border along the wall of the remaining orchard, towards a white 'flowered' *Cornus kousa chinensis*– the flowers in fact being bracts; the yellow-foliaged *Robinia pseudoacacia* 'Frisia', and the silver 'Weeping Pear' *Pyrus salicifolia*, providing an interesting association of colour and form. To the left a long yew hedge divides the lawn from a 'Secret Garden'. Within an alcove formed in this hedge is a striking sculptured head designed by a member of the Shona tribe in 1997 and brought from Zimbabwe. The 'Secret Garden' is entered at the end of this hedge via a terrace with a bench and small shed covered by a Kiwi Fruit *Actinidia chinensis*. The theme of this formal garden is leaf-shape and texture rather than flowers, using such plants as rodgersia, phormiums, ferns and grasses. A gravel path runs the whole length of the garden, broken in the centre with a crossing marked by a *Catalpa bignonioides purpura*, with a small pond to the right. This is a garden of peaceful luxuriance.

## 68 Kingberry

Lanhydrock has had a chequered history since John Robartes built his house in 1635–42, on four sides of an inner court, with a long avenue of sycamores leading up to the gatehouse. In 1758 his successor, following the fashion for bringing the lawn right up to the house, demolished the east wing of the house, opening up the inner court, and leaving the gatehouse isolated and disconnected. He also added a double row of beech trees on each side of the sycamore avenue, and extended the woodland. In the mid-19th century, Thomas James Agar inherited the property. He assumed the name Robartes, and used his great wealth, derived from mining, to improve his estate. In 1857 the fashionable architect George Gilbert Scott, a renowned Gothicist, was employed to extend the ancient dwelling, and reincorporate the gatehouse in the formal gardens beside and in front of the house, which we see today. The Higher Garden behind the house was laid out as a shrubbery at about this time. After a disastrous fire in 1881, the restoration was put in the hands of Richard Coad, of Liskeard, formerly from Scott's office. The seventh Lord Clifden, who inherited the estate in 1930, began replanting the slopes to the rear with ornamental trees and shrubs more in line with current trends than the old Victorian shrubberies. The thatched gardener's cottage, last occupied in 1885, was made a feature, and is now a shelter. He also purchased the splendid bronze urns, designed by Louis Ballin, goldsmith to Louis XIV. Lanhydrock was donated to the National Trust in 1953, and they have added two quadrants to the semi-circular herbaceous border planted in 1914.

69 Lanhydrock

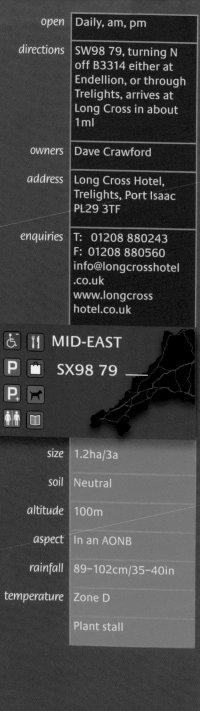

| | |
|---|---|
| open | Daily, am, pm |
| directions | SW98 79, turning N off B3314 either at Endellion, or through Trelights, arrives at Long Cross in about 1ml |
| owners | Dave Crawford |
| address | Long Cross Hotel, Trelights, Port Isaac PL29 3TF |
| enquiries | T: 01208 880243 F: 01208 880560 info@longcrosshotel .co.uk www.longcross hotel.co.uk |

## MID-EAST

SX98 79

| | |
|---|---|
| size | 1.2ha/3a |
| soil | Neutral |
| altitude | 100m |
| aspect | In an AONB |
| rainfall | 89–102cm/35–40in |
| temperature | Zone D |
| | Plant stall |

The house was built around 1900, and is named after the ancient stone cross at the crossroads immediately opposite the north-east gate entrance. The garden was designed by the then owner, a Capt. Allerdyce, with the help of several local gardeners. Subsequently, it fell into decay, although it was still possible to discern the original plan. During the 1980s the then owners began a restoration, which has been continued by their successors. The maze-like nature of the garden might at first sight appear puzzling, until it is recognized that the prevalence of gales from the north coast required both shelter and specialized planting. Several of the Monterey Pines planted as a shelterbelt still survive, and the hedges of escallonia and olearia are salt-tolerant. Below the level of the hedges, it is possible for the more normal species to thrive, and several of the original plants – Welsh poppies, aquilegias and feverfew – have regenerated and self-seeded. Today the borders are again ablaze with herbaceous plants such as lysimachia, lilies, and geraniums. Herbs have become a speciality, and are on sale. The central feature of the garden is an 'ornamental water', with an island decorated with four classical pillars, a statue, and cordylines. Nearby is a 'Mount', opening up a view of the coast, from which at night the lighthouses of Trevose, Hartland and Lundy may be seen. Hidden among the trees is a folly castle from the original garden, and more prominently a modern reproduction dovecote. Long Cross garden is associated with an hotel, which also operates as a tavern with bars and a restaurant for the benefit of visitors.

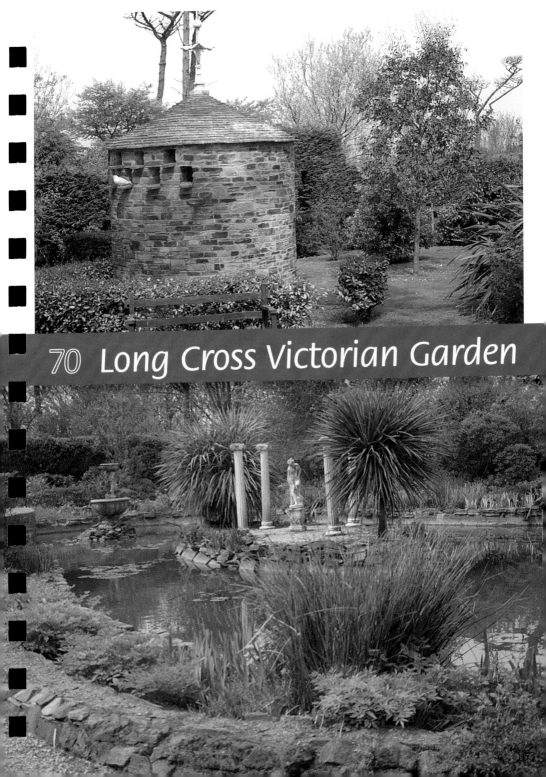

| | |
|---|---|
| open | Daily, excl 24, 25 Dec, am, pm; house and garden private |
| directions | SW99 46, B3273 from St Austell signposted Mevagissey and follow signs |
| contact | Mr Peter Stafford |
| address | Mr Peter Stafford, Heligan, Pentewan, St Austell PL26 6EN |
| enquiries | T: 01726 845100<br>F: : 01726 845101<br>info@heligan.com<br>www.heligan.com |
| pronounced | heLIGan, often anglicized to HELigan |
| EH | House: separate II; kitchen garden walls II |

## MID-EAST

### SW99 46

| | |
|---|---|
| EH | Garden II |
| size | 32ha/80a |
| soil | Lime-free |
| altitude | 95–25m, house 80m |
| aspect | S- and SE-sloping, in an AONB |
| rainfall | 102–114cm/40–45in |
| temperature | Zone D |
| | Plant centre |

The effect of two world wars and social change spelt the end of most great estates. To prevent their total disappearance, in the 1960s the National Trust began to restore gardens, such as **Glendurgan** (38), **Trelissick** (53) and **Trengwainton** (28), as distinct from houses. They were followed by private entrepreneurs, such as Maj. Tony Hibbert at **Trebah** (51). This movement inspired Tim Smit to restore the 'lost' garden of the Tremayne family at Heligan. Both the house and garden had a long history – a quite elaborate, formal garden was swept away in the late 18th century, to be replaced by the landscape seen today. The delapidated walled garden with its glasshouses for grapes, peaches and even bananas, and its pits for pineapples, were the first to be restored, with a working kitchen and flower garden. This was followed by a large, organic vegetable garden, using techniques pioneered by John Harris in the Victorian walled garden at **Tresillian House** (88). Large estates had big families, armies of servants, and regiments of outside workers to feed, and the surplus went to market. The valley, or 'Japanese Garden', now the 'Jungle', and so called from the origin of many of the plants, was tackled next. There was a ravine as well as a rock garden, and a small 'Italian' garden more reminiscent of household gardens in Pompeii than the elaborate statuary and fountain gardens of the Tivoli. Mrs Tremayne planted an 'old-fashioned' herbaceous border in a walled garden. All of these and more were restored to recreate the atmosphere of a typical 19th-century garden. The publicity given to Heligan has led to a welcome increase in enthusiasm for visiting historic gardens, and encouraged further revivals, such as that at **Trevarno** (30).

| | |
|---|---|
| open | Sun all year except Christmas, also Mon, Thu Apr–Sep, am, pm |
| directions | SX11 75, on Bodmin Moor take turning to St Breward off A30 with a cattle grid at the crossroad opposite turning to Temple, and continue 1m bearing R to Bradford. Sculpture Garden is on L |
| owner | Ms Sheila Holland |
| address | Lower Bradford, Blisland, Bodmin PL30 4LF |
| | T:  01208 850195 |

**MID-EAST**

**SX11 75**

| | |
|---|---|
| size | 1ha/2.4a |
| soil | Lime-free |
| altitude | 217m |
| aspect | In a SAGLV |
| rainfall | 102–114cm/40–45in |
| temperature | Zone E |
| | Plant sales |

This is a garden snatched from the open moorland, although not itself a moorland garden. When Sheila Holland arrived here in 1986, this was no more than a flat field. Since then, she has been steadily planting such trees as took her fancy, protected from the winds by an inconspicuous belt of conifers. After her son had moved to town, with advancing years, wild nature began to take over, but following his return, unwelcome intruders such as brambles are being banished. The garden is entered through a courtyard where the sculptures are on view, together with plants for sale. A path leads up to the garden exposing a depression, excavated to relieve the flatness of the site, with paths running around the perimeter, and a central 'island' surmounted with rockwork. The wild and semi-wild plants growing here are generally small, but all around rise the tall trees. The progressive stages of planting have resulted in these and the underlying shrubs being so placed that they are viewed in the round, for this is not a woodland, but a varied and fascinating personal collection, planted to be admired. One enthusiasm has been for eucalypts, many not found in Cornish nurseries – and perhaps not even in many gardens – but which, year by year, have been introduced from specialist nurseries. With their striking bark and strange leaves, they contrast with our more familiar species. This is not a manicured garden; rough paths wind through grassland rich in spring with wild flowers – campion, primroses and foxgloves – with here and there the occasional sculpture. During the season there are also rhododendrons and magnolias in bloom, but this should not deter tree-lovers at other seasons, whose visits will be equally well rewarded.

# 72 Lower Bradford
## Wilderness Sculpture Garden

| | |
|---|---|
| open | Apr–Oct, Sun–Wed, am, pm |
| directions | SX07 54, leave A390 at St Blazey traffic lights, take first L to Par. Over level crossing, garden is on L just before Par station – look for signs |
| owner | Judith Stevens |
| address | Marsh Villa, St Andrews Road, Par, St Austell PL24 2LU |
| enquiries | T:  01726 815920 |

**MID-EAST**

**SX07 54**

| | |
|---|---|
| size | 1.2ha/3a |
| soil | In-filled |
| altitude | River level |
| rainfall | 114–127cm/45–50in |
| temperature | Zone Đ |
| | Plant stall |

The gardens at Marsh Villa have been created out of a former tidal creek, made famous by Daphne du Maurier in her novel *House on the Strand*. It has taken 17 years for the marshland to be consolidated, chiefly with waste soil of no great quality, which, however, belies the great interest and beauty of the garden. The main garden is long and relatively narrow, ending in natural marsh that is a haven for wildlife. Paths wander through areas variously planted with trees, and underplanted with shrubs and the occasional herbaceous border. As one strolls through the various glades, a catalpa and huge contorted willow catch the eye, and a *Cornus kousa* with white bracts; then a paulownia; the evergreen, late-flowering hoheria, followed by the parrotia, one of the few trees to colour well in Cornwall. There are both forms of drimys; a clerodendron, and a Judas tree – a list that merely whets the appetite, rather than exhausts the many other varieties to be seen. At the end of these walks are two areas hedged with escallonia. The first screens a large, natural pond with water-lilies and hovering dragonflies, overlooked by a summerhouse. The second, by way of contrast, encloses a formal garden with two full herbaceous borders running the length of each side, and a third island bed in the centre between them. These have each been expertly and harmoniously planted with contrasting colour schemes. This is a most rewarding garden to visit, of great variety and quality.

# 73 Marsh Villa Gardens

Menacuddle was celebrated for its artificial waterfall, emanating from a well in the floor of the ruined chapel or baptistry, the waters of which 'roll through a narrow dell, darkened with leafage, and strewed with enormous rocks' to flow away under Menacuddle bridge. Gilbert, in his *Historical Survey*, described the scene in 1822 after the garden had been purchased and restored by Charles Rashleigh:

> There is a variety of intricate walks carried through the inclosure; also ponds, stored with fish of gold and silver hues. The upper walks stretch over the steep acclivities, in zig-zag directions, accompanied by rustic seats, formed of rough blocks of wood, covered with moss, and entwined with ivy. Opposite a rustic building called the Hermitage, stands a pedestal, capped with an urn, bearing a profile likeness of the late earl of Mount Edgcumbe.

The grounds later fell into decay, but were restored by Sir Charles Sawle in memory of his son, who was killed in the First World War, and presented to the local authorities as public gardens. Today they have again regressed, but may still be relished by those with an appetite for the eerie isolation of the place, echoing with the rush of tumbling waters.

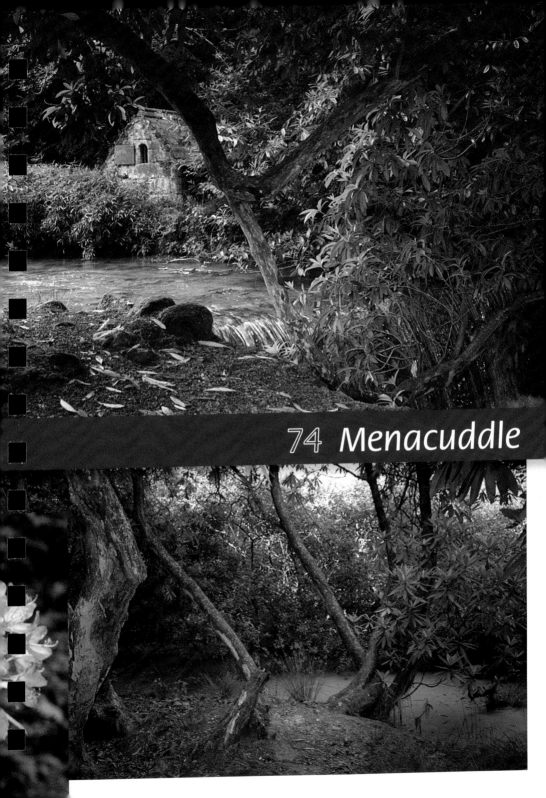

74 Menacuddle

| | |
|---|---|
| open | Apr–Jun, Sep–Oct, Fri, Sat, am, pm, or by arrangement |
| directions | SX01 67, NW on outskirts of Nanstallon turn at sign, nursery 1ml on R |
| owner | Jackie Miller |
| address | Oak Lodge, Cotton Wood, Nanstallon, Bodmin PL30 5LQ |
| enquiries | T: 01208 831292 millres@ compuserve.com www.cotton-wood.co.uk |

**P**
**ii**
**⊼**

## MID-EAST

### SX01 67

| | |
|---|---|
| size | Medium to large in 14ha/35a-woodland |
| soil | Lime-free |
| altitude | From 50m |
| aspect | N-sloping, in a SAGLV |
| rainfall | 102–114cm/40-45in |
| temperature | Zone E |
| | Nursery |

Now a well-planted garden on the edge of Cotton Wood above the River Camel, until the mid-1970s Oak Lodge was an intensive poultry farm. The entry and parking alongside the nursery lead out to a large, sloping meadow which is being developed. This is set amidst natural woods, but many specimen trees have been planted in the open grassland. Near to the entrance a summerhouse has been enclosed with trellis, and planted as a place of repose. At some distance, at the other end of the field near a magnificent mature chestnut and walnut, a matching enclosure with a pergola has been set up for use as a barbecue. Mid-way between the two enclosures has been created a large wildlife pond, edged with candelabra primulas and other water plants, with a projecting viewing platform. Running down from this pond a long gravel channel continues the same theme. There are walks along the river bank, and through the woodland – carpeted with bluebells and wood anemones in season – which has been considerably extended by the acquisition of a further 28 acres (11ha) in 2001. The main ornamental plantations, however, lie on the near-side of the meadow below the nursery, entered past a curved island bed with shrubs and herbaceous plants. The earlier planting around the house consisted predominantly of ornamental trees and conifers, with some underplanting of shrubs, ferns, and other woodland species, through which paths wind on to grassy glades, where the beauty lies in the contrasts of foliage and form. By the house, where teas are occasionally served, a small pond has been created in the Japanese style. The landscaped woods of Oak Lodge echo the natural woodland so characteristic of the Camel valley.

75  Oak Lodge Woodland
Garden & Nursery

| | |
|---|---|
| open | Apr–Oct, daily, excl Wed, am, pm |
| directions | SX06 71, access from A30 1ml N of Bodmin, or from B3266 Bodmin – Camelford road |
| owners | Mr & Mrs R. Whurr |
| address | The Old Mill Herbary, Helland Bridge, Bodmin PL30 4QR |
| enquiries | T: 01208 841206 F: 01208 841206 enquiries@oldmill. herbary.co.uk www.oldmillherbary. co.uk |

**MID-EAST**

**SX06 71**

| | |
|---|---|
| size | 2ha/5a |
| soil | Lime-free |
| altitude | 40m |
| aspect | In a SAGLV |
| rainfall | 102–114cm/40–45in |
| temperature | Zone E |
| | Nuresry: herbs |

Formerly part of the ancient Colquite Estate, the Old Mill is situated alongside the venerable Helland Bridge, the only bridge in the Camel valley, other than that at Wadebridge, to survive the 'Great Flood' of 1847. The corn and saw mill was run from a leat fed by a natural stream, supplemented when necessary by the river. Although still working in the early 1930s, the mill closed and had been demolished before the Second World War. The Herbary was begun in 1984, and opened to the public in 1986, with the leat cleaned and restored to pass beneath a renovated granite clapper bridge, which now feeds a bog garden. The steep sides of the valley sloping down to the river had needed much labour before they could be terraced and cultivated. Brenda Whurr, a former nurse, was drawn to the study of herbal remedies, so that her special interest has been in encouraging wild life and plants, and in collecting rare species for medicinal use, and for the flavouring of food. This semi-wild garden has thus been planted with a wide variety of medicinal, culinary and aromatic herbs, which have attracted many who are interested, or perhaps professionally involved, in kindred subjects. The woodland walks in springtime are carpeted with daffodils, bluebells, wood anemones, and later with ferns, in an area designated as a Site of Special Scientific Interest and a Special Area of Conservation. Among other features are a camomile lawn, a pond with water plants, and a 'Greek Fertility Theme', which in other contexts might be described as for 'adult viewing only'.

# 76 The Old Mill Herbary

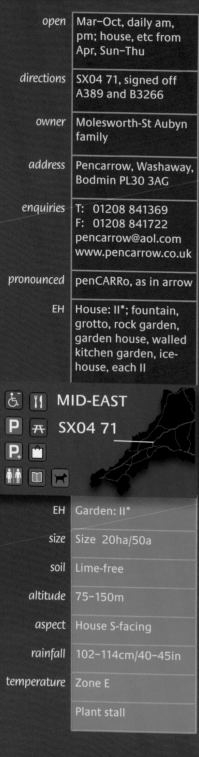

| | |
|---|---|
| open | Mar–Oct, daily am, pm; house, etc from Apr, Sun–Thu |
| directions | SX04 71, signed off A389 and B3266 |
| owner | Molesworth-St Aubyn family |
| address | Pencarrow, Washaway, Bodmin PL30 3AG |
| enquiries | T:  01208 841369 F:  01208 841722 pencarrow@aol.com www.pencarrow.co.uk |
| pronounced | penCARRo, as in arrow |
| EH | House: II*; fountain, grotto, rock garden, garden house, walled kitchen garden, ice-house, each II |

**MID-EAST**

**SX04 71**

| | |
|---|---|
| EH | Garden: II* |
| size | Size  20ha/50a |
| soil | Lime-free |
| altitude | 75–150m |
| aspect | House S-facing |
| rainfall | 102–114cm/40–45in |
| temperature | Zone E |
| | Plant stall |

Once a Domesday manor, Pencarrow was remodelled in about 1844 by George Wightwick for Sir William Molesworth, who as Chief Commissioner of Works had arranged for the opening to the public of Kew Gardens. His popularity with his constituents led to their assisting him in laying out his grounds between his political activities. First, he created the elaborate, semi-elliptical Italian Garden, the central fountain copied from that in the Piazza Navonna in Rome. Corbett, his gardener, on the eastern side simulated a moorland rock-strewn slope, with a cave and grotto. These innovations were followed by planting the main, mile-long (1.6km) drive with trees raised from seed obtained from the mid-century plant hunters, such as William Lobb, Sir Joseph Hooker, and David Douglas, and from Veitch's nursery in Exeter. His last task was to plant up the Green Drive leading to the Camelford Gate; an American Garden of conifers; and rhododendrons and some camellias, under a canopy of beech and elm. Before his death in 1855, Sir William was able to boast that he had planted a specimen of every conifer, save ten, capable of growing in the Cornish climate. The work of planting was continued by his sister, Mrs Ford. It is claimed that it was here that a guest, on seeing his first araucaria – of which there is an avenue at Pencarrow – was the first to remark that 'It would be a puzzle for a monkey'.  The Rounds, an ancient encampment and a Celtic cross are joined by later features such as the lake and wishing well; ice- and palm-houses; the cockpit by the drive, and the ample kitchen gardens. Sir Arscott Molesworth-St Aubyn, who died in 1998, emulated Sir William's extensive planting of conifers, rhododendrons and camellias.

77 Pencarrow

| | |
|---|---|
| open | Mid-Mar–end Oct, daily am, pm |
| directions | SX04 53, signed on A390 E of St Austell between Holmbush and Tregrehan |
| owners | Ray & Shirley Clemo |
| address | Pine Lodge, Holmbush, St Austell PL25 3RQ |
| enquiries | T: 01726 73500 F: 01726 77370 garden@pine-lodge.com www.pine-lodge.co.uk |

MID-EAST

SX04 53

| | |
|---|---|
| size | 12ha/30a |
| soil | Alluvial lime-free |
| altitude | 25–15m |
| aspect | Various |
| rainfall | 114–127cm/45–50in |
| temperature | Zone D |
| NC | Grevilleas |
| | Nursery |

The Lodge was acquired by the present owners in 1974. The first task was to build a formal terrace and sunken garden in front of the house, which led into an informal area of lawns. Next was the creation of winding paths through island beds. By the mid 1980s, these were filled with an increasingly wide range of rare and unusual trees, shrubs and other plants. The area beyond was developed into an arboretum, large enough for the specimen trees not to be cramped, and the accessibility of water facilitated the creation of a quite sizeable lake in a field above the house, planted with water lilies. Next the entrance was improved, with a red brick serpentine pathway through the plantation arriving at the front of the house between two waterfalls, cascading down huge rocks and feeding into a large pond with Koi carp, over which the house is reached by a bridge. The arboretum was extended on one side into a pinetum, where the trees are graded in size eventually to form a semi-circular amphitheatre. The lower side of the arboretum has been retained as parkland, and a new lake, with black swans and wild ducks, has been formed from water from mine workings. The 'Slave Garden' was next to be created – so named from a central feature, around which is a circle of herbaceous beds with graded colours, and a collection of 14 magnolias in the surrounding lawn. The most recent addition has been a Japanese Garden, influenced by a visit to that country. The over 6,000 plants, many rare if not unique, have all been labelled by Mrs Shirley Clemo, who has become an expert plantswoman. This brief account vastly understates the great interest and beauty of this garden which, it has been suggested, possesses the finest and most varied collection of plants in Cornwall.

Mar–Oct, daily am, pm; Nov–Feb, weekends only am, pm

SX12 66, E of Bodmin from A30 roundabout take A38 towards Plymouth, first L to Cardinham and Fletchers Bridge, garden 1.5ml on R

Mark & Claire Woodbine

Pinsla Lodge, Cardinham, Bodmin PL30 4AY

T: 01208 821339
F: 01208 821339
info@
pinslagarden.co.
www.pinsla
garden.co.uk

D-EAST

X12 66

0.6ha/1.5a

Lime-free

145m

In an SAGLV

114–127cm/45–50in

Zone F

Nursery

Situated in the Cardinham Woods, Pinsla in the 17th and 18th centuries had been a deer park attached to the Lanhydrock estate. Today, what is described by the owners as a 'romantic and inspirational' garden surrounds a former lodge of Glynn House, to which they came in 1983. At first, space had to be cut out of the overgrown woodland with an under-growth of laurel. Claire Woodbine – a not inappropriate name in the context! – had formerly worked in the theatrical world, from which she brought an imaginative flair to her designs for the garden. This is almost entirely covered with herbaceous plants and shrub borders, through which wind decorative paths patterned with various slates and cobbles set in con-crete, and forming, with granite boulders, a characteristic feature. The planting provides splashes of contrasting colour, punctuated with dramatic clumps of alliums and yellow rudbeckias. In front, leading from a small rectangular pond, and at the side of the house are mixed beds of low and alpine plants. Sculptures, in the form of painted concrete, and a metal spider and web have been incorpo-rated into the general design. The garden is entered through the nursery, which holds a wide range of plants – over 600 varieties – attractively arranged, many of which, including a good number of ferns and shade plants, are difficult to find elsewhere, and reflect the style of planting in the garden, which is atmospheric and a haven for the plant-lover.

# 79 Pinsla Garden & Nursery

| | |
|---|---|
| open | Several Suns Mar–May, am, pm |
| directions | SX03 50, E on A390 out of St Austell, turn R after Asda, signed to Porthpean, take 2nd L after hospital, signed to Lower Porthpean, entrance on L at bottom of hill |
| owners | Mr & Mrs C. Petherick |
| address | Porthpean House, Lower Porthpean, St Austell PL26 6AX |
| enquiries | T: 01726 72888 |
| pronounced | porthPEAN |
| EH | House: II |

## MID-EAST

### SX03 50

| | |
|---|---|
| size | 1.2ha/3a |
| soil | Shaly, lime-free |
| altitude | From 45m |
| aspect | E-sloping |
| rainfall | 102–114cm/40–45in |
| temperature | Zone D |
| | Plant sales |

The garden at Porthpean, once an inn, was laid out on a low cliff directly above the beach, by Maurice Petherick, in the mid-1950s. There is a panoramic view of the sea, particularly from the top of the garden. At first there was little more than a ragged line of tamarisks to ward off the salt-laden gales. These were replaced by a variety of shrubs and trees – bay, elder, ash and pittosporum. In other parts of the garden there are large, well-established beeches, chestnuts and Monterey pine, to act as windbreaks. Even so, the garden is quite grey with salt after bad gales, and sometimes artificial shelter has to be used. The garden was designed for a collection of camellias, of which some 200 were planted during the first five years. Detailed records of the varieties planted were kept in a card index. A special charm of this garden is the natural carpet of primroses, which are generally in flower at the same time as the camellias.

# 80 Porthpean House Gardens

| | |
|---|---|
| open | Sun–Thu, Easter for 1 week; May–Oct, pm |
| directions | SW91 75, on edge of Padstow, brown signs from ring road (A389) |
| owners | Mr & Mrs Peter Prideaux-Brune |
| address | Prideaux Place, Padstow PL28 8RP |
| enquiries | T: 01841 532411 F: 01841 532945 office@prideauxplace .fsnet.co.uk |
| pronounced | PRIDoh |
| EH | House: I; dairy, grotto, temple, grotto niche, garden seat on terrace, each II*; horse trough, grotto niche, shell house (remains), garden walls, sunken garden, each II |

**MID-EAST**

**SW91 75**

| | |
|---|---|
| EH | Garden: II |
| size | c.2ha/5a + deer park c.2ha/5a, in estate 16ha/40a |
| soil | Lime-free |
| altitude | 55–45m |
| aspect | E-sloping, in an AONB |
| rainfall | 76–89cm/30–35in |
| temperature | Zone D |

184

Nicholas Prideaux purchased the fee-simple of Padstow at the dissolution of the Priory, thus enabling his descendant to build a 'stately house' there in 1592. Edmund Prideaux, who inherited in 1728, made many alterations, redesigning the garden after a visit to Italy in 1739–40. His keen interest in architecture and garden design is evident in a series of sketches made on two tours, in 1716 and 1727, chiefly to the houses of his relatives. His depiction of Prideaux shows along the front of the house the existing long terrace, with central steps between pillars. To the extreme left is a square building, perhaps used to house his 'Roman antiquities', an obelisk, and the temple. In the foreground, below the terrace, is an elaborate formal garden. By 1758, when his son Humphrey succeeded, fashions were changing. Illustrations now show the house as castellated, and the terrace with a central gate-house and embattled with cannon. The obelisk had disappeared, but not the temple. The whole foreground had become a deer park, with a walled garden to the left. This is one of only three deer parks in Cornwall to have survived to the present day, bearing a legend that if the deer were to die out, so too would the family. When the Revd Charles Prideaux-Brune (the 'Brune' was added in response to the will of his maternal uncle) became the owner in 1793, further extensions and alterations were made. The dairy was adorned as a grotto, another being incorporated into the terrace. He continued his rockwork at the stable-yard water trough. The shell house, and the Victorian sunken garden, now restored, and formerly with a handsome conservatory on the end platform, date from 1878 and were designed by Charles Glynn Prideaux-Brune.

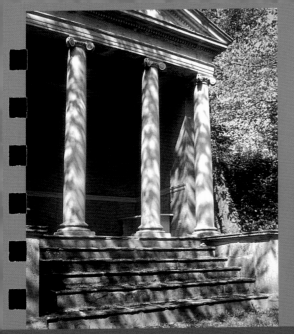

# 81 Prideaux Place

## MID-EAST
### SX11 51

| | |
|---|---|
| size | 0.6ha/1.5a |
| soil | Lime-free |
| altitude | Near shore level |
| aspect | SE-facing valley |
| rainfall | 102–114cm/40–45in |
| temperature | Zone D |
| | Plant stall |

The house is converted from the stables and coach house to the large, Italianate villa at Point Neptune, built by the second William Rashleigh (1817–71). From 1942 to 1943, Readymoney was the residence of Daphne du Maurier, where she wrote *Hungry Hill*, before moving to Menabilly, the model for 'Manderley' in her novel *Rebecca*. Unlike most stables, the building had an attractive front, now in part covered with the double 'Vyvyan Pennell', 'Jackmanii' and 'Polish Spirit', growing through the rose 'May Queen'; a Passion flower, and a 'japonica'; and along the side, an 'Albertine' rose. The front garden in summer glows with pink hydrangeas, but it is the valley to the rear that contains the greatest treasures. A stream runs west of the house, where a bog garden containing arum and 'Day' lilies, candelabra primulas, and ferns, fringed with a carpet of geraniums overlying springtime bluebells, leads up to the sloping sides of the valley, which are closely planted with a variety of mixed shrubs. Below, along the stream and valley bottom, are colourful herbaceous beds. An arbour is draped with the golden hop, a *Clematis orientalis* 'Orange Peel', and an akebia. Nearby is a natural bed of marsh orchids bearing over 50 flowers – a genus that is a speciality of Mr Read, who cultivates the more tender species, with hoyas and other South American plants, in his heated greenhouse. Another speciality is bamboos, of which there are some 25 varieties. It is impossible here to do justice to this fascinating garden, which will be of particular interest to the plant-lover.

# 82 Readymoney Cove

| | |
|---|---|
| open | One Sun each, Jun and Jul, pm |
| directions | SX09 15, 8ml NE of Bodmin. From the centre of St Breward village, go down hill 1ml towards Wenford Bridge. At the first crossroads, after grass triangle with red telephone box, turn L opposite the farm lane. The garden is 800yd on the R, immediately after a dangerous bend |
| owner | Mrs Paddy Powell |
| address | Rose Cottage, De Lank, St Breward, Bodmin PL30 4ND |
| enquiries | T: 01208 850186 |

## MID-EAST
### SX09 15

| | |
|---|---|
| size | 0.4ha/1a |
| soil | Lime-free |
| aspect | Sloping W from 120m, in a SAGLV |
| rainfall | 102–114cm/40–45in |
| temperature | Zone E |
| | Plant sales |

Rose Cottage is the first in a line of cottages that nestle on a bend below the level of the road, protected in a hollow. This colourful garden, bright with white and pink poppies, surrounds these dwellings in a characteristically cottagey, though nonetheless refined style. The sections are arranged not so much in compartments, but as they relate to the individual buildings. In front of Rose Cottage the lawn is small; to the left a small pond is fed by water cascading from an ornamental fish's mouth. Alongside is a silver border, with both shrubby and herbaceous senecios, perovskia and argyranthemums. This leads up to an urn, which forms the focal point of this garden, where steps lead to a gate bordered with a *Rhododendron yakushimanum*, azaleas, camellias, and a tall *Magnolia stellata*. From this point the drive, along which visitors enter, dips down to The Hollow. At the end is a charming detached 17th-century house with mullioned windows, against which grows a *Magnolia grandiflora*. The side, where a pergola is covered with wisteria, faces a triangular lawn. Opposite is the 'Arbour' garden, where the sunny seat looks out over the countryside, and the shady seat is flanked by meconopsis. The path extends down this side through the two long herbaceous borders, with apricot and white foxgloves and a bed of hostas. A *Magnolia wilsonii* has been strategically planted on a bank, where one can look up into the hanging cups of the flowers. On the other side of the lawn, the stream has been shaped into a cascade, so that after rain the sound of babbling water is heard from afar. Rose Cottage has been open locally for eight years, but is now, by request, open to a wider public.

| | |
|---|---|
| open | One Sun Aug, pm, and on request |
| directions | SW91 48, 1ml from Grampound off A390; lane entrance is 100yd W of Grampound Road crossroads and 0.5ml E of Trewithen roundabout |
| owners | Mr & Mrs K.A. O'Connor |
| address | Tregoose, Grampound, Truro TR2 4DB |
| enquiries | T: 01726 882460 |
| pronounced | treGOOSE |

P ☕

## MID-EAST
## SW91 48

| | |
|---|---|
| size | Small to medium |
| soil | Lime-free |
| altitude | 75m |
| aspect | S-facing |
| rainfall | 102–114cm/40–45in |
| temperature | Zone D |
| | Plant sales |

The sight of Tregoose, surrounded by trees, lying below to the left of the road to Grampound just after the entrance to Trewithen, has always been intriguing, and so its opening has satisfied any curiosity about the nature of the garden within. The house was built in 1840 for the agent of the nearby Trewithen estate, although it has since been extended. The grounds were originally laid out in lawns with a shelter belt of mature trees, and have been developed since about 1980 by Mrs O'Connor, who is herself a trained horticulturist. The garden has been planted for all-year interest. At the entrance, one is at once struck by a free-standing *Magnolia grandiflora* 'Goliath', and by fine bushes of camellias, such as 'Freedom Bell' – one of the few red *williamsii*. Another *Magnolia grandiflora* – 'Exmouth' – adorns the front of the house, joined by the climbing, hydrangea-like pilostegia. In the conservatory adjoining the house, the glorious flowers of *Camellia rosiflora* 'Royalty' benefit from the shelter, as do brugmansia and ipomoea. Everywhere the plants are varieties of distinction or rarity – a *Magnolia mollicomata* is a seedling from **Caerhays** (61); a pieris near the house is the recent 'Dorothy Wyckoff' variety; while among the daffodils, the hybrid 'Green Howard' is rarely seen elsewhere. There is also an expanding collection of snowdrops. One of the more recent features is the creation of a potager behind the house. The walled garden is quartered into four herbaceous beds – one overtopped by an *Acacia baileyana* 'Purpurea' – which are colourful in summer.

| | |
|---|---|
| open | Mid-Mar–mid-Jun, Wed–Sun, excl Easter Sun, + bank holiday Mons, am, pm; also Wed only, mid-Jun–Aug, pm |
| directions | SX05 53, entrance on A390 opposite Britannia Inn |
| owners | Mr T.C. Hudson |
| address | Tregrehan, Par, St Austell PL24 2SJ |
| enquiries | T:  01726 812438<br>F: 01726 814389 |
| pronounced | treGRAIN |
| EH | House: II |

**MID-EAST**

**SX05 53**

| | |
|---|---|
| EH | Garden: II* |
| size | 8ha/20a |
| soil | Lime-free |
| altitude | 65–15m, house at 55m |
| aspect | S-facing slope |
| rainfall | 114–127cm/45–50in |
| temperature | Zone D |
| | Plant sales |

Formerly in the possession of the Brodrugans and Edgcumbes, since 1565 Tregrehan has been occupied by the Carlyon family, who extensively planted the parkland during the 18th century. In 1840 the house was remodelled by the Cornish architect George Wightwick for Edward Carlyon, who also invited the up-and-coming Nesfield to design a parterre to the south of the enlarged house, with a new Entrance Court for the West Front. Nesfield's original plan, dated 1843, is still preserved at Tregrehan. His labour-intensive parterres, in the style known as 'broderie', composed of coloured gravel and grass, have now gone, but the terrace in front of the house, with its stone balustrading, urns, and statues of the Four Seasons still survive. The circular pool with its 'charming dolphin fountain', which forms a central feature in the large walled kitchen garden, created at the same time, is also believed to have been designed by Nesfield. This garden, now re-styled, also contains a fine range of greenhouses. Edgar Thurston, in 1930, had written that 'The fine Pinetum is a special feature of the grounds, which contain one of the choicest collections of rare trees and shrubs in the County', reflecting the opinion of W.J. Bean, who had visited Tregrehan in 1916, and it has always been for its collection of trees that Tregrehan has been celebrated. Many of these – now of magnificent size – still survive, among them two avenues of stately yews. Today, there have been added many new specimens from the Southern hemisphere, reflecting the family's interest in New Zealand. In recent years, the garden has also became famous for the camellia hybrids raised by the late Miss Gillian Carlyon.

85 Tregrehan

| | |
|---|---|
| open | At all times; admission free |
| directions | SW81 61, turn R off A392 road to Newquay on to A3028, Trenance is immediately on L |
| owner | Restormel Borough Council |
| address | Trevember and Edgcumbe Roads, Newquay |
| enquiries | T: 01637 854020 |
| pronounced | treNANCE |

**MID-EAST**

**SW81 61**

| | |
|---|---|
| size | Medium size |
| soil | Lime-free and alkaline |
| altitude | At river level |
| aspect | NE–SW valley |
| rainfall | 76–89cm/30–35in |
| temperature | Zone C |

With the growth of the holiday industry in Newquay, the upper part of the Trenance Valley at the rear of the town was laid out in 1906 as a public garden, and the narrow track widened for vehicles. The sunny, sheltered nature of this valley was considered a pleasant contrast for visitors to the more bracing air of the sands and cliffs. The gardens had the advantage – especially in an area that is predominantly alkaline – of having on the slopes a thin, acid soil in which camellias, rhododendrons and heathers could be grown. In 1933 the gardens were extended to provide a large boating lake, a quarter of a mile (0.4km) long, by damming the stream flowing into the Gannel, around which were planted flower gardens. These gardens have been extended into a large leisure area occupying over 16 acres (6.5ha). Today, the slopes have become the site of the Lakeside Café, and most of the area surrounding the lake has been laid to lawn. The islands, however, are furnished with trees, and on the largest are three 'willow men' by Serena de la Hey, looking out into the distant countryside. At the northern end of the lake, on the site of a former nursery, a fine rose garden was planted in 1993, with a pergola, and metal obelisks in the centre of the beds for climbers. This has the great benefit of a permanent plan, by which all the varieties can be easily identified. The formal flower gardens are in a separate area across a side road. Here there is opportunity to relax in a peaceful atmosphere, and to enjoy the colourful bedding schemes.

## 86  Trenance Gardens

| open | End Mar–end Oct, daily excl Tue, Sat; plus Tue mid-Jul–mid-Sep, am, pm |
|---|---|
| directions | SW84 58, from Newquay via A392 and A3058; R at Kestle Mill (NT signposts) |
| owner | NT |
| address | Trerice, Kestle Mill, Newquay TR8 4PG |
| enquiries | T: 01637 875404 F: 01637 879300 trerice@nationaltrust.org.uk www.nationaltrust.org.uk |
| pronounced | TR'RICE |
| EH | House: I (open to public); garden walls and gate-piers, lions, outbuildings, each II |

MID-EAST

SW84 58

| size | 2.4ha/6a |
|---|---|
| soil | Limey |
| altitude | From 30m |
| aspect | W-sloping towards river |
| rainfall | 89–102cm/35–40in |
| temperature | Zone D |
| | Plant stall |

A former Domesday manor, Trerice came by marriage to the Arundells in about 1330. The Elizabethan house was built for Sir John Arundell in about 1570, and was described by Michael Trinick of the National Trust as half-hidden

> by elms, its curving grey gables command no distant view, for this is a close country, and Elizabethan builders cared more for sheltered places, and the presence of pure spring water, than for a wide prospect.

By default of male issue, the estate eventually passed from the Arundells to the Aclands.

Gilbert, in his *Historical Survey* of 1822, found 'little appearance of its once fruitful gardens, raised terrace, and expansive lakes.' The gardens as they are now seen have been laid out since the National Trust came into possession of the house in 1953, but with due regard for the style and antiquity of the site. The forecourt, once probably cobbled, was turfed and planted with borders in 1969; the present garden walls probably date from no earlier than the beginning of the 19th century. From this forecourt, steps lead up north to the bowling green, also a 19th-century addition, with level terraces above, all of a type described by Graham Stuart Thomas as 'nearly unique in Cornwall'. To the south, old illustrations show a 'Dutch Garden', but all signs of this have vanished, and in 1972 this area was planted with herbaceous borders, and an orchard with a collection of old apples, arranged in a *quincunx* pattern, where the trees are in line from whichever angle they are viewed. The Arundell lions, originally from Kenegie near Penzance, were rescued by the National Trust from Lifton in Devon, and brought here for safety. There is an interesting museum of lawnmowers.

| | |
|---|---|
| open | Groups by appointment only |
| directions | SW85 58, A3058 from Newquay 1ml on R past Kestle Mill |
| contact | Mr John Harris c/o Trevarthian Cottage, Kestle Mill, Newquay TR8 4PQ |
| address | Tresillian House, Summercourt, Newquay TR8 4PS |
| enquiries | T: 07979 527840 or 01637 877447 rjohn.harris@btinternet.com www.moongardening.fsnet.co.uk |
| pronounced | treSILLian |
| EH | House: II |

**MID-EAST**

**SW85 58**

| | |
|---|---|
| size | 12ha/30a, in 80ha/200a estate |
| soil | Alkaline |
| altitude | 70–55m |
| aspect | W-sloping |
| rainfall | 89–102cm/35–40in |
| temperature | Zone D |

The core of the present house at Tresillian was built in 1792, and remodelled in 1820, but when Capt. Leonard Bennet inherited his uncle's estate in 1928, he found the house neglected, and the grounds overgrown. This state of affairs he proceeded at once to rectify, by cutting down trees to open up the pond to view; building a greenhouse; erecting a pergola, and planting flowering shrubs. In 1947, after the Second World War, the estate was sold, and in the 1970s became the residence of the owner of the home farm – now a 'theme park' known as 'Dairyland' – who further developed the grounds. In particular, from the late 1980s the walled garden, which dates from the 18th century, was laid out in Victorian style, by the knowledgeable head gardener, John Harris, with old varieties, and plants formerly used as organic remedies against pests and diseases. In 1993, he began a reference collection of 100 varieties of apples – 78 of Cornish origin – interspersed with medlars and quinces, as part of a plan to create at Tresillian an authentic representation of historic gardening practices in the county. Harris's expertise and advice was to prove invaluable during the restoration of **Heligan** (71). The garden at Tresillian is entirely organic, and lunar-orientated.

## 88 Tresillian House Garden

## Bude and North-East Cornwall

Gardens in the extreme north of the county, open to the sea and the ravages of the north and north-west winds, are thin on the ground. For example, along this strip, west of the A39 from Port Isaac to the county border at Morwenstowe, only six places received mention in the historic records as possessing any sort of garden. Moreover, except for Bude, which is not of any great antiquity, and perhaps Camelford, there is no town of substance in the whole of this region north of Wadebridge. This is not to say that there were no settlements or old manor houses in this area; indeed, they were probably just as frequent as in other localities, but they were not in situations that encouraged their development into mansions with parks, or were such as would lead to the creation of new estates during the years of prosperity.

(See gardens 99, 107.)

## Launceston

The dearth of gardens in the previous section, along the exposed western side of Bodmin Moor, was a consequence of the isolation of the region from the mainstream of traffic, and the harsher geographical factors. Here on the eastern side of the Moor, the gardens have been influenced more by the configuration of the rivers that span the area, than by their proximity to Launceston, ancient and important though that town may have been. The Tamar, along the whole of its length, forms the border of Cornwall with Devon, but it has been its tributaries, such as the Ottery, the Inney, and especially the Lynher, which have influenced the distribution of gardens. The Ottery, for instance, flows through **Werrington** (122) to form a distinctive feature and feed a lake, until eventually joining the Tamar close to the borders of the Park. **Penheale Manor** (103), with two lakes, also benefits from streams that run into the Ottery. Launceston itself stands a little west of the

river on another smaller tributary, the Kensey. The greatest of the tributaries – the Lynher – which, by the time it meets the Tamar at its mouth, will have swollen sufficiently to have become its rival, begins as a trickle flowing down from the Moors, and rushes as a cataract into the grounds of **Trebartha Hall** (108) to feed the swan pond. More peaceably, a few miles south at **Berriow Bridge** (91), the village gardens are opened every other year.

(See gardens 91, 96, 103, 108, 109.)

Bude
Launceston
Liskeard

# 5 EAST

## Liskeard and South-East Cornwall

This final section covers a broad area of interior, coastal and riverside landscape, dissected by river valleys that make communications roundabout and difficult. Such towns as there are tend to serve areas confined within natural boundaries, each with its own characteristics and local justification. To the west, Liskeard, once with a castle and two deer parks, lies at the head of the long valley of the East Looe river, which opens into the sea almost due south. **Moyclare** (102), on its outskirts, has an interesting contemporary garden. To the east of Looe is St Ger-

man's, where the River Lynher opens out into the Tamar to form the twin estuary of the Hamoaze. Here is **Port Eliot** (119), one of the two gardens in mainland Cornwall with an English Heritage Grade I for national significance. East of St German's, towards Saltash and Torpoint, the great natural beauty of the landscape has given birth to many parks and gardens, chief among them **Mount Edgcumbe** (101), the other of the Grade I gardens, and along the Tamar **Antony** (89), **Ince Castle** (97), **Pentillie** (118), and **Cotehele** (92).

*(See gardens 89, 90, 92, 93, 94, 95, 97, 98, 100, 101, 102, 104, 105, 106, 107.)*

| | |
|---|---|
| Apr–Oct, Tue–Thu, + bank holiday Mons + Sun Jun, Jul, Aug, pm | |
| SX41 56, entrance off A374 on outskirts of Torpoint | |
| NT | |
| Antony House, Torpoint PL11 2QA | |
| T: 01752 812364<br>F: 01752 812364<br>antony@nationaltrust.org.uk www.nationaltrust.org.uk | |
| House: I (open to public); dovecote II*; kitchen garden walls, claire-voie, bath house, dovecote (remains), each II | |

EAST

41 56

Garden: II*

10ha/25a

Lime-free, medium loam on shale

60m–sea; house 25m

NW-sloping to sea, in a SAGLV

89–102cm/35–40cm

Zone D

600 Day Lilies (*Hemerocallis*)

The Domesday manor had a long history before the arrival there of the Carews in the late 15th century, of whom the most celebrated was Richard Carew, author of the first *Survey of Cornwall* (1602). The present house was built between 1711 and 1721 on a new site. A sketch of the garden front by Edmund Prideaux in 1727 shows the dovecote, which still survives, and an elaborate, formal walled garden with radiating avenues beyond. This formality was swept away on the recommendation of Humphry Repton, who prepared a 'Red Book' in 1792. In the 19th century, the *porte-cochère* was added to the front of the house, and vistas were cut through the perimeter belt of trees to Shillingham on the other side of the river. The first yew walks were begun, and were extended in the 20th century. It was at this time that the garden's reputation began to grow. The family were encouraged and assisted in the development of the garden by J.C. Williams of **Caerhays** (61) and Lionel de Rothschild of Exbury, which led to the introduction of a great variety of azaleas, rhododendrons and magnolias. An enclosed Summer Garden was begun in 1983 by Lady Mary Carew Pole, who also designed the Knot Garden. A National Collection of 600 Day Lilies (*Hemerocallis*) was assembled by the present Sir Richard's mother, Lady Cynthia Carew Pole. Antony House was donated to the National Trust in 1961, and the Trust has continued to develop the garden. A number of modern sculptures have been sensitively introduced, including *Hypezlone* by Simon Cook (p. 203). The management of the original woodland at Antony has been separated (see 90).

# 89 Antony House & Garden

Mar–Oct, daily excl
Mon and Fri, but open
bank holidays, am, pm

SX41 56, entrance off
A374 on outskirts of
Torpoint

Carew Pole Garden
Trust

Antony House,
Torpoint PL11 2QA

T:  01752 812364
F:  01752 812364
paulcressy@
stratton-
holborrow.co.uk

EAST

41 56

40ha/100a woodland

Lime-free, medium
loam on shale

From 60m to river
level

NW-sloping, in a
SAGLV

89–102cm/35–40in

Zone D

*Camellia japonica*

The extensive woodland gardens were not taken over with **Antony** House and formal garden (89) by the National Trust, but have remained separately managed by the Carew Pole Garden Trust. Since 1984, Sir Richard Carew Pole, who was elected President of the RHS in 2001, has been involved in its ongoing development. The woodlands may be visited on their own, or there are various routes from the garden, along wandering pathways designed to reveal the many beauties and vistas from the woods. In spring the glades are carpeted with primroses, bluebells, campions, and the beautiful but pungent wild garlic. Spring is also the season first for camellias – of which Antony has a National Collection of *C. japonica* – and the magnolias, planted in the 1950s, for which Sir Richard has a special enthusiasm. There is a named collection of 103 magnolias at Antony. The northern edge of the Woodland Gardens is marked by Jupiter Point, so named from the figurehead of a ship once placed there, but now decayed. In its place is a large granite stone in memory of Sir John and Lady Cynthia Carew Pole, who were responsible for so much of the planting over the last 50 years, which bears an apt inscription from *Omar Khayam* – 'And still a garden by the water blows'. There are rhododendrons to follow, and acers, which are at their best later in the year; while the many varieties of conifer maintain their beauty and interest throughout the year. There are over 6,000 plants in the Antony list, and these woodlands will provide a feast for the tree-lover.

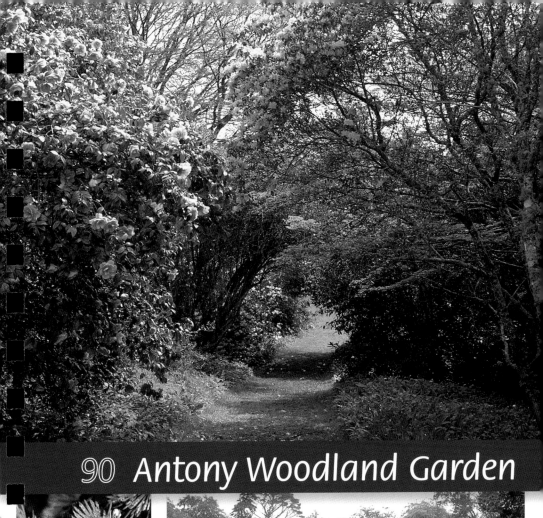

# 90  Antony Woodland Garden

| | |
|---|---|
| open | One Sat, Sun in summer, alternate years (open 2004); occasionally at other times |
| directions | SX27 75, situated where B3254 crosses River Lynher between Launceston and Liskeard |
| organizer | Mrs J. Bousfield |
| address | Hillbrook, Middlewood, North Hill, Launceston PL15 7NN |
| enquiries | T:  01566 782661, or see NGS annual yellow book or www.ngs.org.uk |

P

EAST

SX27 75

| | |
|---|---|
| size | A group of small village gardens |
| soil | Lime-free |
| altitude | c.130m |
| aspects | Various |
| rainfall | 127–152cm/50–60in |
| temperature | Zone F |
| | Plant sales and Bregover Nursery |

For many years, the ancient bridge over the River Lynher at Berriow, with the neighbouring hamlet of Middlewood, has been the scene of a biennial garden festival, which has been featured on television. From a suggestion by Jenny Bousfield, it was initiated and organized by Myra and Tony Frith, then of Berriow Bridge House, where Tony Frith had planted an orchard and two-acre (0.8ha) woodland. The gardens participating in the festival tend to vary, but in 2002 as many as 11 – six in Berriow, and five in Middlewood – took part. The trail begins at **Berriow Bridge House**, where, together with **Chy Berrio**, to which the Friths have moved, the garden has been landscaped since 1979, with rockeries, terraces, and a water garden along the river frontage. At Berriow Bridge House an apple-crusher stands as a central feature, and at Chy Berrio there are many intriguing stone and wooden sculptures by Tony Frith. Across the road, another garden, **Heortnesse**, has an acre (0.4ha) of moorland garden, which contrasts pools, waterfalls and granite boulders with a kaleidoscope of shrubs and flowers. The **Middlewood** gardens tend to be on a smaller scale, but each with its own individual attractions. The trail ends at the cottage garden at **Hillbrook** where there is an art studio, and the **Bregover Plants Nursery**.

## 91  Berriow Bridge & Middlewood Gardens

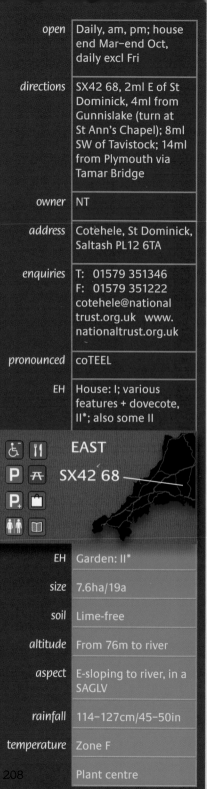

**EAST**

**SX42 68**

Pevsner judged Cotehele to be 'the most extensive and important Tudor house of Cornwall'. The old house, of which remnants remain in the lower walls, was remodelled for Sir Richard Edgcumbe and his son Piers in the late 15th century. Norden's map of *c.* 1690 shows two deer parks, and the medieval dovecote still survives. The oak and chestnut trees, which are of great antiquity, although scarcely the 1,000 years suggested by a writer in 1842, regularly caused 'astonishment', and in 1799 the yews were reckoned to be 'some of the largest ... in England'. The Edgcumbes transferred to **Mount Edgcumbe** (101) in about 1553, after which Cotehele was no more than an occasional residence. The house was again remodelled in about 1862, when the terraces were laid out 'in old-fashioned beds and borders filled with hardy flowers'. In more recent years, since Cotehele has been in the care of the National Trust, the gardens have been greatly developed. Below the terraces, and across the road in the upper valley garden, are the dovecote, a 19th-century summerhouse, and a small lake, which was probably the medieval stew-pond. Below, the lower valley becomes densely wooded, with clearings and pools with shrubs and water-loving plants. In the upper garden, to the north-east of the house, there is a square pond with lilies, and nearby an orchard. It was noted in 1893 that: 'This place' was 'the centre of very extensive fruit gardens, hundreds of acres being devoted to Cherries, Strawberries, Raspberries, Plums, &c.', although not all, of course, on the Cotehele estate itself.

## 92 Cotehele

The garden at East Down Barn, along a lane on the outskirts of Menheniot, has been created since 1992 on a slope dropping sharply down to a stream in a narrow valley. On the level by the house is a bank, and a large circular bed by the front entrance crowded with alpines and the smaller herbaceous plants, such as campanula, geraniums, and the daisy-flowered *Erigeron* 'Profusion'. On the bank, the curious cerinthe with grey leaves and striking blue flowers catches the eye. The steep, almost precipitate slope has been terraced and planted with mixed borders of cistus, lavenders, poppies and foxgloves. Several large specimens of the 'Beauty Bush' *Kolkwitzia amabilis* stand out when flowering profusely. Leading on to a narrow lawn is a rustic pergola, covered by clematis, roses and the golden hop, alongside which is a novel gravel bed with ornamental grasses and other spiky plants. In a corner grows the handsome tiered *Cornus contoversa*, sometimes called the 'Wedding Cake Tree'. The lawn runs down to a boggy area by the stream, over which is a wooden bridge. Here the natural planting includes as well as wild grasses and ferns, the candelabra primulas. Valerie Sturdy was a finalist in the BBC television programme 'Gardener of the Year 2000', and winner of the Garden Knowledge Challenge Section. This garden displays an interesting range and combination of plants, and the very difficult site has been managed in an expert way, which will serve as an ideal model for those who face similar problems.

## 93 East Down Barn

| | |
|---|---|
| open | 1st Sun in month, Apr–Sep, am, pm; other Suns on request |
| directions | SX18 73, from Jamaica Inn off A30 at Bolventor, take road south to Colliford Lake and St Neot, 2.5ml to Higher Gillhouse |
| owners | John & Iris Stanton |
| address | Higher Gillhouse, St Neot, Liskeard PL14 6PY |
| enquiries | T: 01579 320789 irisstanton@ hotmail.com |

**EAST**

**SX18 73**

| | |
|---|---|
| size | 1.2ha 3a |
| soil | Lime-free |
| altitude | 265m |
| rainfall | 114–127cm/45–50in |
| temperature | Zone F |
| | Plant sales |

At 870ft (265m) altitude, Gillhouse is the highest garden in Cornwall, but although it is set in moorland it is not moorland in character. Mr Stanton, who came here with his wife in 1988, had worked as head gardener in several places, including Haseley Court in Oxfordshire – a far cry from Bodmin Moor. An early attempt to grow trees was unsuccessful, but now, chiefly with herbaceous and lower-growing plants sheltered by hedges, it has proved possible to create a flourishing and colourful garden. The position, sloping gently down to the shores of Colliford Lake, opens up several vistas across to the tors of the high moor. Upon entering, the garden radiates in three directions. In the centre, a granite path leads up to the house, alongside which a colourful herbaceous border nestles against the hedge. From the top of this hedge can be viewed a surprising V-shaped parterre, filled principally with red-leafed begonias, with contrasting edging. On the right, a moorland stream that runs underground has emerged to channel itself into a small pool before again draining away. At the top of the path, nearer the house, an enclosed area suitable for sitting and relaxing is ablaze with colour – crocosmias; the 'Bishop of Llandaff' dahlia; blue ligularia, and other bright plants. The garden continues to the south with island beds, a small pool, and an immaculate vegetable garden with tunnels, to complete an unexpected display in a spectacular setting.

94 Gillhouse Garden

| | |
|---|---|
| open | 2 Sats in Aug, pm |
| directions | SX43 62, turn off A388 between St Mellion and Hatt signed to Cargreen; nursery in village next to Chapel, where facilities are located |
| owners | Mr & Mrs B.J. Richards |
| address | Highcroft Gardens, Cargreen, Saltash PL12 6PA |
| enquiries | T: 01752 842219 |

EAST

SX43 62

| | |
|---|---|
| size | 0.8ha/2a |
| soil | Neutral, sandy loam |
| aspect | N-sloping from 45m, in a SAGLV |
| rainfall | 114–127cm/45–50in |
| temperature | Zone E |
| | Plant sales |

This garden, created over the last 20 years, was described as a 'relaxation' from the daily tasks in a market garden (not open to the public) with extensive greenhouses, specializing in some 28 varieties of alstromerias. The entrance drive arrives at the front of the house, where a new rock garden has replaced some overgrown shrubs. Hidden to the rear is a 'Japanese' garden with a summerhouse and pergola covered with wisteria, where a serpentine rill runs through the paving to a central pump. Since the flow of water became problematic, the rill has been filled with intense blue glass chippings, the colour being taken up by the surrounding blue pots filled with agaves. The front lawn, with two large island beds with herbaceous plants – spurge, zebra grass and sedum – is backed by evergreen shrubs, camellias, and the variegated pieris, to provide all-year colour. Gravel paths lead out from this home garden, threading their way through wide beds of mixed plantings of shrubs and herbaceous plants designed to produce spectacular combinations of colour – a 'hot bed' of reds and oranges; the Cotinus 'Royal Purple' against Lonicera 'Baggesen's Gold'; silver perovskia against Cornus alba 'Aurea'. A long gravel path, with arches of clematis, runs the whole length of this garden, with a roofed 'lych' gate leading out into the lower garden, through which, on looking back, the chapel can be seen in the distance. The lower slopes, where the path is bordered with hydrangeas, is being planted with specimen trees, while the path back to the nursery passes through a collection of buddlejas. This sensational garden was featured in *Devon Life* in 2002, and is due to appear in *Gardens Illustrated*. It is one of the few Cornish gardens at its height in the summer.

## 95  Highcroft Gardens

| | |
|---|---|
| open | One Sun each in Apr, May, Jun, pm |
| directions | SX30 85, take Egloskerry turn out of St Stephens; first L to Truscott |
| owners | John Mann |
| address | Higher Truscott, St Stephens, Launceston PL15 8LA |
| enquiries | T: 01566 772755 |

EAST

SX30 85

| | |
|---|---|
| size | 0.4ha/1a |
| soil | Neutral |
| altitude | 170m |
| aspect | S-sloping |
| rainfall | 102–114cm/40–45in |
| temperature | Zone G |
| | Plant sales |

This garden, as its name suggests, is set at a high altitude, sloping gently to the south, but exposed to damaging winds from the east. Higher Truscott is an old long-house with later farm buildings. The garden was originally created in 1966 in the yard of this old farm, as an adjunct to be viewed from the house. Nearby, there has been an attempt to grow alpines in gravel, rock beds and troughs, which has not always been successful in this climate, but a small greenhouse in a courtyard serves as an alpine house. Across a lawn, at the farther end of the house garden, trees and shrubs have been planted – camellias, rhododendrons and magnolias, with underplantings of fritillarias and hellebores. The soil here is shallow and stony, so that plants suffer from both wet and dry spells. In 1980 a second garden was begun across the road in a field, which, although if anything more exposed, has a fine view beyond Launceston Castle all the way to Dartmoor. This has provided an opportunity to develop island beds with herbaceous plants, to create colour in the summer. Beyond the summer garden is the kitchen garden, which by way of contrast is of a formal design, with beds edged with box or herbs, in which the vegetables and fruit are neatly arranged. John Mann is a keen and knowledgeable gardener, a member of the Hardy Plant Society, and a committee member of the Cornwall Garden Society.

## 96 Higher Truscott

| | |
|---|---|
| open | One Sun each in Apr–Jul, pm |
| directions | SX40 56, from A38 at Stoketon Cross take turn signed to Trematon; continue along road signed to Elmgate and Saltash to lane to Ince |
| owners | Viscount & Viscountess Boyd |
| address | Ince Castle, Saltash PL12 4QZ |
| enquiries | T: 01752 842249 F: 01752 847134 boydince@aol.com |
| pronounced | INS as in 'instant' |
| EH | House: I |

**EAST**

**SX40 56**

| | |
|---|---|
| size | 2ha/5a |
| soil | Lime-free shale |
| altitude | From 25m |
| aspect | N- and SE-sloping to river, in a SAGLV |
| rainfall | 102–114cm/40–45in |
| temperature | Zone D |

Although an ancient site, the remarkable series of gardens at Ince have been created only since 1960, by the late Viscountess Boyd and her husband. On entering from the car-park, the 'Summer Garden' aglow with fiery herbaceous plants leads on to the swimming pool, with stone obelisks at each corner, and a panoramic view across the Lynher river. Proceeding towards the south front of the house, we arrive at three gardens, the lower being the lily pond, which has at each end a lead *putto* riding upon a snail. At the western end, the interior of the 'Shell House' glistens with a mosaic of exotic shells. From the lily pond, the house is seen beyond the formal garden, quartered by paths with obelisks echoing the theme at the swimming pool, the four beds filled with herbaceous plants. Beyond is a wide paved area with a central tank and fountain. Off to the right, the more recent 'Castle Garden' is also quartered, with lawns of camomile, thyme and pink and white thrift, while nearby, from the 'Mound', is a distant view of Plymouth. To the left of the paved area, a long path leads towards the kitchen garden, with the tennis court on the right. There are two paths richly planted on each side with deep mixed borders. North of the house is the woodland garden, with a wide variety of trees, where an oval glade opens on to a water garden. There is a dovecote, among other features, many of which were brought from the courtyard of Lady Boyd's father's house in St James's Square, London. Ince is among the premier contemporary gardens in Cornwall.

| | |
|---|---|
| open | Mid-Apr–end Sep, Sun–Fri, am, pm |
| directions | SX31 69, from A390 to Callington turn off N at Butchers Arms, St Ive; take Pensilva road; at next crossroad take road signed Bicton |
| owners | Mr & Mrs K.R. Willcock |
| address | Ken-Caro, Bicton, Liskeard PL14 5RF |
| enquiries | T: 01579 362446 |
| | KEN CARo as in arrow |

P
P₊
[accessibility/toilets icon]

EAST
SX31 69

| | |
|---|---|
| size | 1.6ha/4a |
| soil | Very acid |
| altitude | 175m |
| aspect | E-sloping, in an AGLV |
| rainfall | 114–127cm/45–50in |
| temperature | Zone F |
| | Plant sales |

Ken Caro is set high above Bicton Manor and Woods, whose former deer park is reflected in its name. The garden, begun in 1970, was created around a small bungalow, protected from the wind by high hedges. Some 20 years later it began to be extended into the meadow beyond. This was followed by the erection of a more substantial house, dressed with neatly planted bedding. The new garden of four acres (1.6ha) has been designed on rather different lines from the original, but with the same skill in the selection and association of plants by Mrs Willcock and her husband Kenneth, who is well known for his floristry, and writes a regular column in the *Cornish Gardener*. The new garden is more open; laid out in sweeping island beds, arranged to lead the eye out into the distant landscape, and with a summerhouse at a strategic high point. The beds are mixed shrub and herbaceous plantings, wide enough for paths to thread through them for a closer look. Everywhere the care in plant associations is evident – a *Ligularia* 'Yellow Rocket' contrasts with a purple berberis; a *Rubus* 'Gold Vale' enhances the intense blue of a *Ceanothus* 'Concha'. There are various other features in the garden: a circular pergola enclosing a small raised pool is clothed with honeysuckle and roses; at a higher level, a large pond affords an opportunity to grow bog and water plants. There is even a small bed devoted to insectivorous plants, with nearby a curious natural 'sculpture' made from driftwood, and another by the pond. Ken Caro will interest the plantsman, but cannot fail to delight everyone.

98 Ken-Caro

| | |
|---|---|
| open | Two Suns in Jun, pm |
| directions | SX05 84, on B3314 turn L at Westdowns from Pendoggett, or R from Delabole, signposted to Treligga. Turn L after entering village, Long Hay 30yd on L with white gate. Park in farmyard |
| owners | Bett & Mick Hartley |
| address | Long Hay, Treligga, nr Delabole, Camelford PL33 9EE |
| enquiries | See NGS yellow book, or www.ngs.org.uk |

P ☕

**EAST**

SX08 63

| | |
|---|---|
| size | 0.3ha/0.75a |
| soil | Neutral |
| altitude | 130m |
| aspect | In an AONB |
| rainfall | 89–102cm/35–40in |
| temperature | Zone E |
| | Plant stall |

On entering the tiny front garden of Long Hay – a small, cottage-style garden set in a remote village near the north coast – the house is seen half-shielded by a shapely juniper. A *Phlomis fructicosa* grows out of the hedge at the gate, and the bed curving around to the rear has a variety of unusual plants, among them an exochorda, which flowers in the spring. To the rear of the house, the mixed herbaceous beds are dense with a variety of colourful plants, topped by delphiniums and lupins. In the midst of these beds is a small pool. Mrs Hartley has added to her more conventional gardening interests a love of succulents, so there are the hardy sempervivums and the less hardy agaves, echeverias and aeoniums scattered about in pots and on window sills. The kitchen garden and small orchard, which are across a meadow, nearer the cliffs, should on no account be missed. Those with no interest in vegetables will be recompensed by the spectacular view along the coast from Tintagel church to Lundy, and Port Isaac Bay and Pentire Point, even to Trevose headland.

## 99  Long Hay

| | |
|---|---|
| open | By arrangement |
| directions | SX43 58, Culver Road is near the town centre, and leads to the Town Quay |
| owner | Tamar Protection Society |
| address | Mary Newman's Cottage, Culver Road, Saltash |
| enquiries | T: 01579 844846 |

EAST

SX43 58

| | |
|---|---|
| size | 0.2ha/0.5a |
| soil | Neutral |
| altitude | Near river level |
| aspect | In a SAGLV |
| rainfall | 102–114cm/40–45in |
| temperature | Zone E |

In 1568, when 17 years old, Mary Newman married Francis Drake at St Budeaux Church, Plymouth, where she lies buried. The tradition that she lived in this house was already accepted by 1820, and there is no reason to believe otherwise. There had been dwellings here since the 12th century, although the present house appears to date from the 15th or 16th century, perhaps incorporating earlier material. The site has been described as originally a 'burgage plot' – one on which vegetables might be grown and a cow kept, customarily in size some 50 x 115ft (15 x 35m). The present garden is laid out in a typical cottage style of a much later date. It is divided into three sections – that nearest the house is a herb garden, while the middle section is a lawn, with borders, and an arbour from which there is a view of the river and its bridges. Indeed, it has been romantically suggested that from an upper window-seat in the cottage, Mary could have seen her husband's ship rounding the headland into harbour. In the third section, paths wind through beds of roses, herbaceous and other plants, some, as the old-fashioned roses, with appropriate names – 'Sir Walter Raleigh', and 'William Shakespeare', and a green santolina brought from Sudeley Castle, where it is said that Kathryn Parr had used the plant from her herb garden to ease Henry VIII's legs. The Cottage has been restored and is maintained by the Tamar Protection Society.

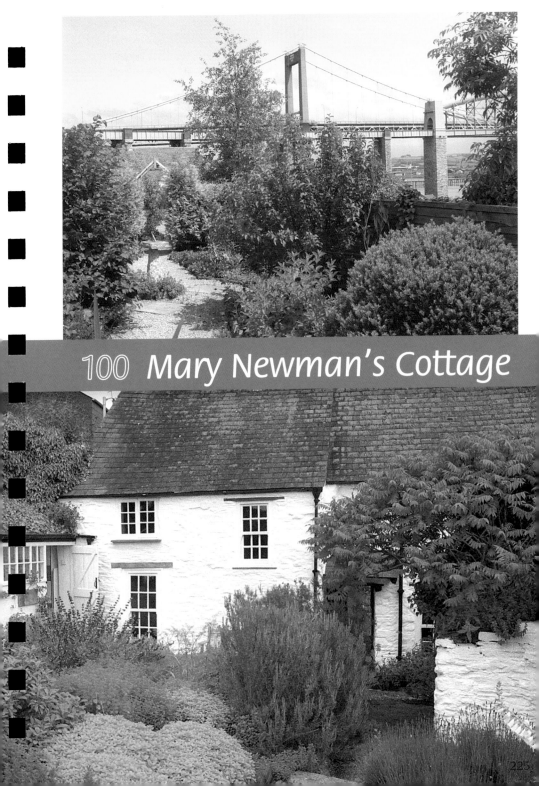

# 100 Mary Newman's Cottage

**EAST**

**SX45 52**

The commander of the Armada vowed he would take over Mount Edgcumbe after victory and, by the 18th century, it had become required viewing for persons of fashion, including Dr Johnson, Horace Walpole, Samuel Pepys, and David Garrick. The Edgcumbes, while resident at **Cotehele** (92), first emparked deer here in 1515, only later moving residence, building a house unprotected and exposed to view, flaunting their high station to one and all. There is no illustration of the garden until that of Badeslade in 1737, which shows an elaborate and grand landscape. One part, laid out as an amphitheatre of trees, was thought to have inspired Milton in describing the 'Walls of Paradise' in his epic, so that a 'Temple of Milton' was built there. The 'Wilderness', near where the ferry now lands, was cut down in the 18th century, opening the way for the wife of the first Earl to lay out the English Garden, joined later by a French Garden, and most elaborate of all, an Italian Garden with orangery, fountain, and double steps with statues. More recently a geyser garden has been added

to commemorate the family's connection with New Zealand. All of these are open to view. Entrance to the house is charged, but is recommended since it includes the reconstructed Earl's Garden. The Earl's walk leads to the Cedar Lawn with its exquisite Shell Seat, encrusted with exotic shells believed brought back by Captain Cook, who often anchored in the bay below. Here too is one of the original lime trees planted in the mid-16th century.

# 101 Mount Edgcumbe House & Country Park

| | |
|---|---|
| open | Strictly by appointment only |
| directions | SX24 63, 0.5ml S from Liskeard centre on St Keyne/Duloe road (B3254), 200yd past station, garden on L |
| owners | Mr & Mrs P. Henslowe |
| address | Moyclare, Lodge Hill, Liskeard PL14 4EH |
| enquiries | T: 01579 343114<br>F: 01579 347948<br>elizabethhenslowe@ btopenworld.com |

EAST

SX24 63

| | |
|---|---|
| size | 0.4ha/1a |
| soil | Lime-free |
| altitude | 100m |
| rainfall | 114–127cm/45–50in |
| temperature | Zone E |

Built in 1927 by Mrs Moira Reid and her husband, Moyclare takes its name from a combination of Moira and Co. Clare, where Mrs Reid was born. Although in a 'frost-pocket', by the 1970s the garden had reached its peak, becoming 'the most televised garden in Cornwall'. Mrs Reid was surprised and flattered to be asked to contribute to Alvilde Lees-Milne and Rosemary Verey's book *The Englishwoman's Garden*, although she had already written articles in the RHS *Journal*, and been visited by many celebrities, including Margery Fish, with whom she shared a love of variegated plants. A seed given her by J.C. Williams of **Caerhays** (61) became *Camellia williamsii* 'Moira Reid'; a *Eucalyptus gunnii* arrived as a gift from Beverley Nicholls, and John Betjeman was reprimanded for calling her Irish-woman's garden 'typically English'! In one article, 'Cramming them in', she wrote: 'I never want to see any bare earth at all'. This has created problems for Mrs Henslowe, who came to live here in 1997, after her aunt's death. Much was overgrown, and the more delicate plants were smothered. A rigorous programme of rehabilitation aims at retaining the spirit of the garden – its informality, with paths meandering through a succession of beds, making the garden appear larger than it is – but there are some new features. Two of these are a pergola covered with golden hop, and a rectangular pond bordered by astilbes. Louis Reid, Moira's husband was a friend of the poet W.B. Yeats, and a line from his poem *He Wishes for the Cloths of Heaven*, peculiarly applicable to this garden, is inscribed on a memorial slate – 'Tread softly for you tread on my dreams'.

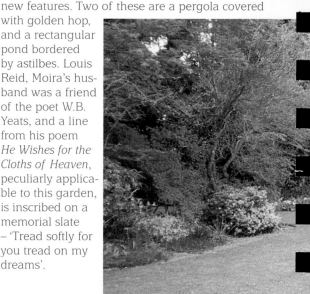

EAST

X26 88

The magnificent stables at Penheale were built by Sir John Specott in 1620, his son Paul completing the house on his marriage in 1636. The front court is entered through a remarkable gatehouse and loggia. Two similar courts above the house, enclosed by a wall, have pavilions at both ends and a raised walk. In 1867 a writer pronounced this to be 'one of the finest and best preserved specimens of ancient manorial residences in the county'. But by 1920, when it was acquired by Capt. Norman Colville, it was dilapidated. His admiration for Castle Drogo in Devon inspired him to engage Sir Edwin Lutyens to restore the house, and Lutyens also designed the parterre next to the house, when Gertrude Jekyll's advice was requested on the planting. The courtyard gardens were extended by the attachment of a square plat approximately four times their size. This similarly was quartered into four 'rooms' enclosed by high yew hedges, reminiscent of those at Castle Drogo. Along the house and extending to the full width of this plat, is a raised walk, lined both above and below by long herbaceous borders, designed by the late Mrs Colville and her gardener. At the end of a parallel grass path, midway between the four rooms of the parterre, steps lead down to a long lake or canal, possibly created out of medieval stew ponds, and ending in woodland planted with camellias and rhododendrons. This insistent formality of squares and long axes is unique in Cornwall, and curiously impressive, especially in conjunction with the quite exceptional planting of the long herbaceous borders along the raised walk, the yew hedges by the house, and at the far edge of the plat.

# 103  Penheale Manor Gardens

| | |
|---|---|
| open | One Sun each in Apr, May, Jun, Jul, Sep, pm |
| directions | SX42 52, from garage in Millbrook follow road to mini-roundabout and turn L. Straight ahead up St John's Rd, Peterdale is last house on L; sign on wall next to house. Park in road |
| owner | Mrs Ann Mountfield |
| address | Peterdale, St John's Road, Millbrook, nr Torpoint PL10 1EE |
| enquiries | T: 01752 823364 |

**EAST**

**SX42 52**

| | |
|---|---|
| size | Very small |
| soil | Neutral |
| altitude | From 30m |
| aspect | NE-sloping, in an AGLV |
| rainfall | 76–89cm/30–35in |
| temperature | Zone D |
| | Plant stall |

A small, suburban bungalow in a modest-sized garden, which rises quite steeply at the back, Peterdale has been the scene of a succession of remarkable, and widely acclaimed gardens. In the mid-1980s it began as a quite conventional garden, although it was clear from the plant associations and general design that here was something above average. The garden was soon developed to a degree where, despite its size, it received a grading in the *Good Garden Guide* comparable to several grander and better-known Cornish gardens. More recently it has undergone an even greater transformation. On arrival, the hedge of purple cotinus, yellow eleagnus, fuchsia and other colourful combinations augur well – the front garden is indeed beautifully planted. But on turning into the rear garden, one enters another world – that of a Feng-Shui garden, representing the eight enrichment methods. At first, as in Chelsea theme gardens, it is the colour of the hard landscaping that strikes the eye – dark blue, turquoise and yellow, with white walls. There is a pergola and vine along the house, and a circular enclosure with a ring of bench seats facing a central feature with mosaics, from which a tall datura (*Brugmansia*) grows. The plantings – trachycarpus, cannas, phormiums, and other exotics – are in walled beds. By way of contrast, the next garden, which is Mediterranean, is minimalist – yellow gravel, white walls, blue metal chairs, and a few spiky plants. This leads up the steeper ground to a densely planted Japanese garden, with two pools, a bridge, and a tea house. This garden won the RHS Rose Bowl for best family garden in Britain. If you missed it on television, do not fail to visit for real.

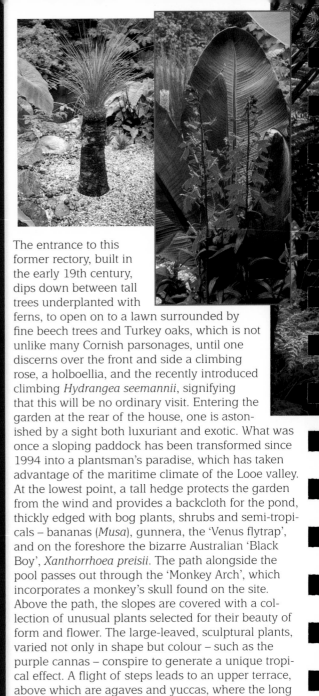

One Sun in Jul, pm, or by request

SX25 55, from Looe B3253 towards Plymouth, L to church almost opposite Looe Garden Centre. Alongside church. Facilities are in church hall

Dr K. Olson & Mr H. Cave

St Martin's Manor, St Martin-by-Looe PL13 1NX

T: 01503 262825

EAST

X25 55

1.6ha/4a

Neutral to lime-free

75–65m

W-sloping

102–114cm/40–45in

Zone E

The entrance to this former rectory, built in the early 19th century, dips down between tall trees underplanted with ferns, to open on to a lawn surrounded by fine beech trees and Turkey oaks, which is not unlike many Cornish parsonages, until one discerns over the front and side a climbing rose, a holboellia, and the recently introduced climbing *Hydrangea seemannii*, signifying that this will be no ordinary visit. Entering the garden at the rear of the house, one is astonished by a sight both luxuriant and exotic. What was once a sloping paddock has been transformed since 1994 into a plantsman's paradise, which has taken advantage of the maritime climate of the Looe valley. At the lowest point, a tall hedge protects the garden from the wind and provides a backcloth for the pond, thickly edged with bog plants, shrubs and semi-tropicals – bananas (*Musa*), gunnera, the 'Venus flytrap', and on the foreshore the bizarre Australian 'Black Boy', *Xanthorrhoea preisii*. The path alongside the pool passes out through the 'Monkey Arch', which incorporates a monkey's skull found on the site. Above the path, the slopes are covered with a collection of unusual plants selected for their beauty of form and flower. The large-leaved, sculptural plants, varied not only in shape but colour – such as the purple cannas – conspire to generate a unique tropical effect. A flight of steps leads to an upper terrace, above which are agaves and yuccas, where the long tentacles of *Beschorneria yuccoides* droop over each side. A garden not to be missed when it comes to life in summer, when so many Cornish gardens are dying down, St Martin's Manor has been featured in the *English Garden* magazine.

# 105  St Martin's Manor

| | |
|---|---|
| open | One Sun each, Jun, July, pm |
| directions | SX21 62, from A38 at N end of Dobwalls follow the sign to Duloe, Herodsfoot and Looe for 1.5ml. Turn R at sign for Scawn; continue for 1ml down to the river |
| owners | Mrs A. Ball & Dr Julian Ball |
| address | Scawn Mill, nr Liskeard PL14 4GS |
| enquiries | See NGS annual yellow book, or www.ngs.org.uk |

P
☕

## EAST

SX21 62

| | |
|---|---|
| size | Medium |
| soil | Lime-free |
| altitude | 65m |
| aspect | In a SAGLV |
| rainfall | 114–127cm/45–50in |
| temperature | Zone E |
| | Plant sales |

The Corn Mill around which the present garden has been created dates back 300 years. Water was taken from the West Looe river to be fed into two mill-pools to drive the wheel. The mill was rebuilt at least twice in its lifetime, but fell into disuse and disrepair after the 1920s, until the more recent partial restoration of the building. Over the years two new woodlands have been planted – the more distant Larch Wood replaced that of scrub oak in 1964; the Penpoly Wood leading from the house was planted in 1992, from a mixture of 7,000 beech and Scotch pine seeds. Around the house are various areas of planting, begun in 1977 – a tennis court below the house, and a Japanese garden leading into the wood. On the other side of the road are a croquet lawn and a fish pond, leading on through woodland underplanted with candelabra primulas to the lake by the larch wood. This was dug down to rock level and waterproofed. A path runs around the lake, which has been planted with Japanese flowering cherries, azaleas and rhododendrons, bamboos and pines, each making their contribution throughout the seasons to the picturesque reflections in the still waters of the lake.

## 106 Scawn Mill

| | |
|---|---|
| *open* | One Sun each Mar, May and Jul, am, pm. Private visits by appointment |
| *directions* | SX20 99, 5ml S of Bude off A39 at Bangors Cross Roads (chapel on corner). Turn into Vicarage Lane, signed to Poundstock church, c.200yd on L |
| *owners* | Mr P.R. & Mrs J.A. Marfleet |
| *address* | Southfield, Vicarage Lane, Poundstock EX23 0AU |
| *enquiries* | T: 01288 361233 |

EAST

SX20 99

| | |
|---|---|
| *size* | 1.25ha/3a |
| *soil* | Lime-free |
| *altitude* | 100m |
| *aspect* | S-sloping, in an AONB |
| *rainfall* | 102–114cm/40–45in |
| *temperature* | Zone E |
| | Plant sales |

In an earlier guise, Southfield featured a collection of some 40 minority breed of fowl, with pigs and goats, which eventually attracted 10,000 visitors a year. This was brought to a sudden halt by the notorious salmonella and listeria scare of 1994, even though there were no cases in Cornwall. Mr and Mrs Marfleet, forced to retrench, began to recreate their land into a garden. The bungalow faces south over a sloping lawn with a terrace, pond and small bed in front, from which there is a fine view of the surrounding countryside. A large herbaceous border down the left side of the garden divides off the kitchen garden, which runs the whole length of the lawn. This is matched on the other side of the lawn by an orchard of fruit trees, among which is the old-fashioned medlar. At the bottom left-hand corner of the lawn, an arch covered with golden hop leads out into a plantation stretching the whole width of the upper garden, in which there is a wide variety of native trees – several forms of oak, beech, rowan, and spindle among others. Beyond this the plantation grades down into natural woodland above a stream. Where the path winds around the tree collection, it is bordered by an underplanting of rhododendrons and other shrubs. In particular, distributed along the sides are 22 distinct varieties of hydrangeas, which make a colourful spectacle, especially where the path turns into a small glade. Alongside the varied interest in this garden is the added attraction of home-made produce on sale, and, when open all day, the opportunity for a light lunch.

## 107 Southfield

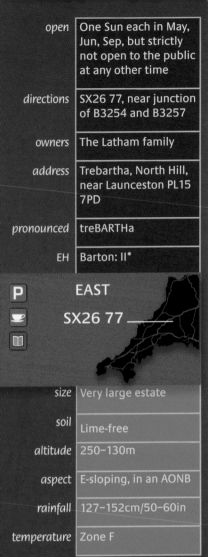

| | |
|---|---|
| open | One Sun each in May, Jun, Sep, but strictly not open to the public at any other time |
| directions | SX26 77, near junction of B3254 and B3257 |
| owners | The Latham family |
| address | Trebartha, North Hill, near Launceston PL15 7PD |
| pronounced | treBARTHa |
| EH | Barton: II* |

**EAST**

**SX26 77**

P

| | |
|---|---|
| size | Very large estate |
| soil | Lime-free |
| altitude | 250–130m |
| aspect | E-sloping, in an AONB |
| rainfall | 127–152cm/50–60in |
| temperature | Zone F |

A sketch of about 1690 shows Trebartha with an elaborate garden full of statues in an Italianate style. This was swept away in the 18th century by Col. Rodd, who erected on its site what Gilbert considered 'a large tasteless building', although with 'good gardens ... surrounded by extensive plantations' through which a torrent roared down from the moors above. Trebartha found a place in Loudon's gazetteer of 1822, and 50 years later was described as 'the best and most stately seat in the county'. It was these plantations, probably planted by Edward Hearle Rodd in the early 19th century, which led the Latham family in 1941 – a time of import shortage – to take advantage of the timber, by purchasing the property. The 'American Gardens', and Upper Terraces were probably mid-19th-century, when many new varieties were becoming available from plant collectors. The Swan Pool, whose boathouse has recently been restored, is landscaped with other interesting specimens, and dates from the beginning of the 20th century. A mound of earth over a nearby grotto-like cave serves as a Mount for viewing the lake. The house, maligned by Gilbert, became delapidated during occupation in the Second World War, and was demolished in 1948. A well in the level parkland has been surrounded by a collection of ancient crosses and mile-stones. The word 'magical' has become a cliché when applied to Cornish gardens, but the stillness of the Swan Pool, broken only by the distant roar of the torrent and the sighing of the great trees that tower up the slopes above, induces an atmosphere to which this over-used word is not inapplicable. Trebartha is a private estate, open only on charity days, and in which there are no rights of way.

| | |
|---|---|
| open | One Sat, Sun in May, pm. Private visits welcome, Jun, Jul |
| directions | SX33 84, follow signs for Leisure Centre along Dunheved Rd. At College end of road take sharp L bend; immediately after, take another L turn into Windmill Hill. Trenance is c.200yd on L. Park in road |
| owners | Mr & Mrs John Dingle |
| address | Trenance, Windmill Hill, Launceston PL15 9AG |
| enquiries | T:  01566 772067 |
| pronounced | treNANCE |

EAST

SX33 84 ————

| | |
|---|---|
| size | 0.5ha/1.75a |
| soil | Lime-free |
| altitude | 180m |
| rainfall | 102–114cm/40–45in |
| temperature | Zone G |
| | Plant sales |

The two acres (0.8ha) at Trenance form an unusually large garden for a town house, although in a road where there are other large gardens. Windmill Hill, as its name implies, is high above the town, and the entrance to the house, lined with mature rhododendrons and camellias, opens up a vista to the countryside beyond. The sloping site has been terraced and planted to provide interest throughout the year. Above the house is a lawned area with a long herbaceous border, a small 'cottage garden', and a collection of hollies. Opposite the house is a formal courtyard garden. Below are a series of gardens surrounding a lawn tennis court, including herbaceous beds and borders, an enclosed slated garden of colourful perennials, an area of heathers and conifers, and a 'winter border'. Ballard *Hellebores* are a speciality of Trenance, as are hardy geraniums, of which there are over 100 varieties distributed throughout the garden.

## 109 Trenance

This book is a guide to gardens that are reliably open to the public. However, there are a substantial number of fine gardens in Cornwall that open occasionally, but not on a regular basis. Among these are more than half the gardens listed by English Heritage as of national significance, and all but one of the gardens for which Humphry Repton produced Red Books between 1792 and 1810. They are therefore mentioned below, out of general interest, and in order to complete the gazetteer. However, the question arises, 'How can I know when they will be open?' There is no simple answer. Typically, these gardens open for charities, parish festivals or other occasions, which are generally advertised only locally, and perhaps not long in advance. Those wishing to visit such gardens are advised to keep a watch on local papers, and to listen to local radio programmes. The diocesan monthly *The Coracle*; the monthly magazine *Inside Cornwall*, and the two free papers *The Cornish Country Gardener* and *The Cornish Gardener*, which can be found in nurseries, all contain up-to-date information.

# 6 Historic Gardens Open Occasionally

For the purposes of cross-reference, these gardens are numbered in sequence with those in the main gazetteer.

## 110 Bosahan
### SW76 25 Manaccan
Bosahan (pronounced 'Bosain') is one of the principal 19th-century valley gardens, created by Sir Arthur Pendarves Vivian. P.D. Williams of Lanarth described it as 'one of the most happily chosen garden sites in Cornwall'. There are two converging valleys running down to the sea, which became celebrated for their early plantings of *Chamaerops, Trachycarpus,* a *Phoenix canariensis*, and tree ferns. The garden (above) is open to groups, strictly by appointment only. (T: 01326 231351.)

## 111 Catchfrench Manor
### SX50 59 St Germans
Catchfrench probably derived its name from the Norman French *chasse franche* – 'free warren' – in the 13th century, when the Cornish purchased from the king the right to hunt. Repton was introduced to Francis Glanville, an MP of William Pitt's party, by Richard Pole Carew of Antony (89). He recommended plantations to give privacy to the house, and the opening up of a prospect by the removal of earth. The garden is EH-listed Grade II, and has been open until a recent change of ownership.

## 112  Chyverton
SW79 51 Zelah

Chyverton was listed EH II after it was recognized as a classic 18th-century landscape – unusual in Cornwall – with a bridge over a serpentine lake, and a Folly as an eye-catcher, originally 'Hunter's Lodge', but later separated as a residence then known as 'Tinker's Castle'. In recent years, since it was purchased in 1924 by Treve Holman, it has become renowned for its trees and shrubs, many collected and introduced by his son Nigel. It is particularly well known for its magnolias. Open to groups strictly by appointment. (T: 01872 540324.)

## 113  The Downes
SW55 36 Trelissick Road, Hayle

The Downes was designed by Edmund Sedding, and the garden by his brother John Dando Sedding, author of *Garden Craft Old and New* (1891), a book that influenced both Thomas Mawson and Edwin Lutyens. It is EH-listed Grade II, as the only surviving work of this high Victorian designer's style. The Downes has been the convent of a nursing order in association with St Michael's Hospital, but its future after sale cannot be foretold.

## 114  Enys
SW79 86
Mylor Bridge

Enys (right) was the first garden in Cornwall to receive public notice, in a Creation play of *c.*1450. Its beauty was later remarked in the 1709 edition of Camden's *Magna Brittania*. The walls and pavilions are still extant, and the lakes in the valley are atmospheric. J.D. Enys, who had sent back seeds and specimens from New Zealand, introduced to this country the beautiful 'Chatham Island Forget-me-not', *Myosotidium hortensis*. In 1907 he privately published a list of some 1,000 *Trees and Shrubs and Plants Growing at Enys*. The plantations suffered greatly from the gales in the early 1980s. The garden is EH-listed Grade II, and is often open at bluebell time.

## 115  Lamellen
SX05 77  St Tudy

The house at Lamellen, a Domesday manor, was built in 1849 by John Penberthy Magor, but it was his son, E.J.P. Magor, who in 1901 seriously applied himself to gardening there, obtaining seed from E.H. Wilson's expeditions and himself joining Reginald Farrer collecting alpines in Switzerland. He was celebrated for his many rhododendron hybrids, especially between Himalayan species – 'Damaris' and 'Lamellen' probably being the best. His son, Maj. Walter Magor, followed his lead, becoming editor of the *Rhododendron Yearbook*, and chairman

als. Although Menabilly is EH-listed Grade II, sadly much has now been lost and the grotto vandalized.

### 118  Pentillie Castle
SX40 64  Pillaton

Pentillie – a castellated house, never a castle – overlooks the River Tamar. Repton, who visited here on the recommendation of Pole Carew of **Antony** (89), admitted in his Red Book of 1810 that he was unfamiliar with this type of terrain. The major outcome from his visit was the remodelling of the house by his associate, William Wilkins, in an 'ecclesiastically Gothic style', possibly with assistance from his son. These additions were demolished in 1968. Loudon included Pentillie in his *Encyclopoedia* gazetteer of 1822. It is EH-listed Grade II, and has been opened, but not recently.

### 119  Port Eliot
SX35 57  St Germans

Port Eliot was the first estate in Cornwall to be visited by Humphry Repton in 1792, by reason of Eliot's relationship by marriage to William Pitt the younger, who had consulted him in 1791. Repton suggested in his Red Book that the house might be joined to the Abbey; this and many other of his recommendations were not taken up, but reappeared in some of the proposals of Sir John Soane for the house. There are also sketches for alterations to the garden thought to be by W.S. Gilpin, but never followed. Port Eliot appears in the gazetteer of Loudon's *Encyclopoedia* as a 'show-place', and is EH-listed Grade I. This fine garden is open occasionally to the public.

of the RHS Rhododendron and Camellia Group, receiving the Veitch Memorial Medal in 1987. Lamellen (above) is EH-listed Grade II, and is still well maintained by the family.

### 116  Lismore House
SW65 27 Cross Street, Helston

This large garden of one of the houses in the fashionable Cross Street, built in 1835, is EH-listed Grade II for its picturesque features – a small serpentine pond, a 'bark' house, a rustic, grotto-like rock arch, and a coach-house ornamented with a cornice, vases and a parapet, intended as an 'eye-catcher' from the house. The procession on Flora Day, in May, passes through this garden.

### 117  Menabilly
SX10 51  near Fowey

Menabilly is the principal seat of the Rashleigh family of Fowey, and in 1822 the garden was described in the gazetteer in Loudon's *Encyclopoedia* as a 'show-place'. It was the model for 'Manderley' in Daphne du Maurier's novel *Rebecca*, and for a time she resided here. It was once celebrated for its collection of bamboos – 'probably as comprehensive as any in the country'; its rare conifers, some from Kew, in 'Hooker Grove'; and a grotto garnished with specimens of Cornish miner-

## 121 Trewarthenick
SW90 44 Tregony

Trewarthenick was visited by Humphry Repton during his excursion in 1792, for which he produced his Red Book in 1793. His recommendations for separating the farm from the house approach; for hiding the service buildings, and breaking up the central avenue have generally been followed. Nevertheless, Trewarthenick remains a forgotten garden, even though it is EH-listed Grade II. It has since developed and is being maintained, but although occasionally open recently, it seems again to have withdrawn into its shell.

## 120 Tregothnan Botanic Gardens
SW85 41 St Michael Penkivel

Tregothnan (above), the residence of Viscount Falmouth, overlooks the River Fal. It was visited by Humphry Repton in 1809, and one of the recommendations in his Red Book was that this vista should be opened up. However, perhaps the most outstanding result of Repton's visit was the remodelling of the house by the younger William Wilkins, son of his former friend, in a Regency style based on the Tudor manor of East Barsham and the Rectory of East Snoring in Norfolk. The house was later enlarged by Lewis Vulliamy in 1845–8, with railings, an arched double lodge at Tresillian Bridge, and a four-mile (6.4km) scenic drive along the River Tresillian. The deer-park is one of the three surviving in Cornwall. The garden, which is EH-listed Grade II*, is richly planted, and the gardener has recently been on several horticultural expeditions. Tregothnan remains a private estate, but further information may be obtained from www.tregothnan.com.

## 122 Werrington Park
SX33 87 near Launceston

Werrington (below) is important first because there is circumstantial evidence for the influence of William Kent by way of Nicholas Morice's marriage to Catherine, daughter of the Earl of Pembroke, who was active in the Palladian circle. There was a Palladian-style bridge; a ruined castle; a temple of the sun; a triumphal arch 'on the model of that on Sidon Hill at Highclere'; a hermitage 'like that at Richmond', and a reproduction of the Tomb of the Horatii at Albano. Most of these have gone or are ruinous. Later, after its purchase by J.C. Williams of **Caerhays** (61) in 1882, Werrington became a repository for the overflow especially of rhododendrons received from expeditions supported by the family, particularly those of Forrest. The garden is EH-listed Grade II, and opens occasionally.

Cornwall is well supplied with nurseries, several of which specialize in varieties of plants that may be difficult to find elsewhere. However, this list provides as wide a conspectus as possible of what is available from one end of the county to the other. It is divided into three sections:

1 *Garden centres*, which supply a variety of gardening and leisure items, as well as plants.

2 *Nurseries associated with the gardens in the Guide*, where further information will be found. Most gardens sell plants when they are open, but those listed are permanent nurseries, open to the public even when not visiting the garden. Among them, 'plant centres' are smaller than 'nurseries', which in some cases are substantial.

3 *Plant nurseries*, whose focus is upon plants rather than horticultural necessities.

# Nurseries & Garden Centres

The garden centres and nurseries that are asterisked are those which contribute to the *RHS Plant Finder*. Note that the garden nurseries feature strongly in this context. It is not possible here to include descriptions of all the nurseries, but where notes are added it is in order to identify those that specialize.

## 1 Garden centres

**Brooks Nurseries & Garden Centre,** Stratton, Bude EX23 9NR. T: 01288 352879. F: 01288 356159.

**\*Burncoose Nurseries,** Gwennap, Redruth TR16 6BJ. T: 01209 860316.

F: 01209 860011. E: burncoose@eclipse .co.uk. W: www.burncoose.co.uk. *Extensive range of over 3,000 ornamental trees and shrubs. Rare and unusual magnolias and rhododendrons.*

**Camborne Garden Centre,** North Roskear Terrace, Camborne TR14 8PR. T/F: 01209 613819.

**Carnon Downs Garden Centre,** Quenchwell Road, Carnon Downs, Truro TR3 6LN. T: 01872 863058. F: 01872 862162.

**Chacewater Garden & Aquatic Centre,** Three Milestone Road, Chacewater, Truro TR4 8QG. T/F: 01872 560533. E: Chacewatergardencentre@netline.uk. net. W: www.chacewatergardencentre. co.uk; www.plantsmailorder.co.uk.

**Cornish Garden Nursery,** Perranarworthal, Truro TR3 7PE. T: 01872 864380. F: 01872 864561.

**\*The Duchy of Cornwall Nursery,** Cott Road, Lostwithiel PL22 0HW. T: 01208 872668. F: 01208 872835. E: sales@ duchyofcornwallnursery.co.uk. W: www. duchyofcornwall nursery.co.uk. *Very wide range of all garden plants, including trees, shrubs, conifers, roses, perennials, fruit, and half-hardy exotics.*

**Falmouth Garden Centre,** Swanpool Road, Goldenbank, Falmouth TR11 5BH. T/F: 01326 315404. E: falmouthgardencentre@.co.uk W: www.falmouthgardencentre.co.uk.

**Golden Bank Nursery & Garden Centre,** Plymouth Road, Liskeard PL14 3PB. T/F: 01579 348622.

**Goonhavern Garden Centre,** Newquay Road, Goonhavern, Truro TR4 9QQ. T/F: 01872 575088.

**Homeleigh Garden & Aquatic Centre,** Dutson, Launceston PL15 9SP.

T: 01566 773147. F: 01566 773547.
E: home@.co.uk.
W: www.homeleighgardencentre.co.uk.

Looe Garden Centre, Pendrym, St Martin's, Looe PL13 1HX. T: 01503 263866.

Newquay Garden Centre, Quintrell Downs, Newquay TR8 4LG. T/F: 01637 872199.

Pengelly Plant Centre, Hewas Water, St Austell PL26 7JG. T: 01726 882428. F: 01726 883757.

Rising Sun Nurseries & Garden Centre, Harrowbarrow, Callington PL17 8JD. T: 01579 351231.

St Austell Garden Centre, Boscundle, St Austell PL25 3RJ. T: 01726 812197. F: 01726 812283.

Tamar View Nurseries Garden Centre, Callington Road, Carkeel, Saltash PL12 6TH. T: 01752 847366. F: 01752 840992.

Trelawney Garden Leisure, Sladebridge, Wadebridge PL27 6JA. T: 01208 812966. F: 01208 814798. W: www.trelawney.co.uk.

Tresillian Garden Centre, Tresillian, Truro TR2 4BA. T/F: 01872 520544.

*Trevena Cross Nurseries & Garden Centre, Breage, Helston TR13 9PD. T: 01736 763880. F: 01736 762828. E: sales@trevenacross.co.uk W: www. trevenacrossnurseries.co.uk. *Specialities: South African and Australasian plants, aloes, proteas, tree ferns, palms, restios – wide range of other and hardy exotics.*

Wyevale: Lelant, Nut Lane, Hayle TR27 6OG. T: 01736 753731. W: www.wyevale.co.uk.

Wyevale: St Austell, Par Moor Road, St Austell PL24 2SQ. T: 01726 814854. W: www.wyevale.co.uk.

## 2 Nurseries associated with gardens

*Bosvigo (34), Truro.

*Bregover Plants, Middlewood (91), *see*

*below under 'Plant Nurseries'.*

*Burncoose (6), nr Redruth.

Carwinion Bamboo Garden (36), Mawnan Smith. T: 01326 250258. F: 01326 250903.

Cotehele Plant Centre (92), nr Saltash.

Glendurgan Plant Centre (38), Mawnan Smith.

Hidden Valley Nurseries (65), Treesmill, nr Par.

Japanese Garden & Bonsai Nursery (67), St Mawgan.

*Lanhydrock Plant Nursery (69), nr Bodmin.

Oak Lodge Nursery (75), nr Bodmin.

*Old Mill Herbary (76), nr Bodmin.

*Pine Lodge Nursery (78), nr St Austell.

Pinsla Garden & Nursery (79), nr Liskeard.

*Roseland House Nursery (20), Chacewater.

*Trebah Enterprises (51), Mawnan Smith.

*Tregothnan Nursery (120), *see below under 'Plant Nurseries'.*

Trelissick Plant Centre (53), Feock.

Trelowarren Plant Centre (27), Mawgan.

Trengwainton Plant Centre (28), Penzance.

*Trewidden Nurseries (31), nr Penzance.

*Trewithen Nurseries (56), nr Truro.

## 3 Plant Nurseries

*Note: Nurseries listed without postcodes do not usually trade by mail order.*

Bay Tree Nurseries, Long Lane, St Hilary, Penzance TR20 9EF. T: 01736 763635.

B.J. Plants & Herbs, Heamoor, Penzance. T: 01736 363763. *Specializes in camellias.*

Blackacre Nurseries, Blackacre, nr Indian Queens. T: 01637 881300.

*Bodmin Plant & Herb Nursery, Laveddon Mill, Lanival Hill, Bodmin PL30 5JU. T: 01208 72837. F: 01208 76491. E: CHYROSE44@aol.com.

*Bregover Plants, Hillbrook, Middle-
wood, North Hill, nr Launceston PL15
7NN. T: 01566 782661.

Brighton Cross Plant Centre, Grampound
Road, Truro. T: 01726 882807.

Calamazag Nursery, East Taphouse,
Liskeard. T: 01579 321799.

Carne View Farm Tree Nursery, Mount
Hawke, Truro. T: 01209 891591.

*Churchtown Nurseries, Gulval, Pen-
zance TR18 3BE. T/F: 01736 362626.

Churchtown Nursery, Perranarworthal,
nr Falmouth. T: 01872 863033.

Crankan Nurseries, Newmill, Penzance.
T: 01736 362897. *Specializes in pelargoniums.*

Croft Farm Plant Centre, Newquay Road,
Goonhavern, Truro. T: 01872 572310.

Cross Common Nursery, The Lizard,
Helston. T: 01326 290722. *Specializes in
half-hardy and exotic varieties.*

Fentongollen Bulb Farm, Merther
Lane, Truro TR2 4AQ. T: 01872
520209. F: 01872 520606. E:
james@flowerfarm.co.uk.
W: www.flowerfarm.co.uk. *Bulb sales
Aug–Dec.*

*Fir Tree Farm Nursery, Tresahor, Con-
stantine, Falmouth TR11 5PL.
T: 01326 340593. E: ftfnur@aol.com.
W: www.cornwallgardens.com.
www.members.aol.com/ftfnur. *3,500
different perennials, and 130 clematis.*

Godolphin Hill Nursery, Godolphin, Helston TR13 9TQ. T: 01736 762124.
E: marshall@euphony.net.

Gweek Nurseries, Chapel Hill, Gweek,
Helston. T: 01326 221311.

Halamanning Nurseries, St Hilary, nr
Penzance. T: 01736 762593.

*Hardy Exotics Nursery, Gilly Lane,
Whitecross, Penzance TR20 8BZ.
T: 01736 740660. F: 01736 741101.
W: www.hardyexotics.co.uk. *Largest
collection of trees, shrubs and herbaceous
plants for tropical and desert effects in
the UK.*

Heather Lane Nursery, Back Lane, Can-
onstown, Penzance. T: 01736 714522.
F: 01736 741294.

J.R. Nurseries, Rosenannon, St Wenn.
T: 01637 880108.

Kelhelland Horticultural Centre, Kelhelland, Camborne TR14 0DD. T: 01209
612445. E-mail enquiries@Kelhellandh
ort.co.uk. W: www.kelhellandhort.co.uk.

Leire Nurseries, Ruan High Lanes, nr
Truro. T: 01872 501502.

Losowek Herbs, Treventon, Well Lane,
St Keverne, Helston TR12 6LZ. T: 01326
280514.

Lower Kennegy Nurseries, Rosudgeon,
Penzance. T: 01736 765929. *Specializes
in agaves and other succulents.*

Myrtle Nursery, High Lane, Manaccan.
T: 01326 231604.

*The Old Withy Garden Nursery, The
Grange, Gweek, Helston TR12 6BE.
T: 01326 221171. E: WithyNursery@fsb
dial.co.uk.

Pentewan Valley Nurseries, Pentewan
Road, St Austell. T: 01726 842360.

Penventon Nursery, Cumford, Lanner,
Redruth. T: 01209 820049.

Peter G. Paris, Boskenna Nurseries, St
Buryan. T: 01736 810384.

Plantation Nursery, 16 New Road, Barip-
per, Camborne. T: 01209 714522.

*Quality Daffodils, 14 Roscarrack Close,
Falmouth TR11 4PJ. T/F: 01326
317959. E: rascamp@daffodils.uk.com.
W: www.daffodils.uk.com. *Specializes in
narcissus hybrids and species. Mail order.*

Rainbow's End Nuseries, Trescowe Common, Germoe, nr Helston. T: 01736
850322.

*Rezare Nurseries, Rezare, nr Trebur-
ley, Launceston PL15 9NX. T: 01579
370969. E: REZARENURSERIES@
aol.com.

*Rosewarne Collections, Duchy College, Rosewarne, Camborne TR14 0AB. T: 01209 722151. F: 01209 722159. E: r.smith@cornwall.ac.uk. *Speciality, National Collection of escallonia hybrids and species.*

Sunny Corner Nurseries, Old Market Garden Centre, Chacewater, Truro. T: 01872 560084.

Tartendown Nurseries, Landrake, Saltash. T: 01752 851431.

Towan Camellia & Hydrangea Nursery, John Price, Mawnan Smith, Falmouth TR11 5HF. T: 01326 251115.

Trebarwith Valley Nursery, Trewarmett, Tintagel PL34 0ET. T: 01840 770625.

*Tregothnan Nursery, Estate Office, Tregothnan, Truro TR2 4AN. T: 01872 520325. F: 01872 520291. E: bigplants@tregothnan.co.uk. W: www.tregothnan.com. *Specializes in rare and unusual plants from own stock, with known-provenance, large specimens.*

Trenowth Nurseries, Lower Trenowth Farm, St Columb. T: 01637 881473.

*Tresidder Farm Plants, St Buryan, Penzance TR19 6EZ. T: 01736 810656. *Specializes in Proteaceae, Aloeacae – large aloe collection, unusual succulents.*

Wall Cottage Nurseries, Lockengate, St Austell. T: 01208 832234.

# Calendar of Garden Openings

## 1   Gardens open all year

Barbara Hepworth Museum (4), St Ives

Boconnoc (59) nr Lostwithiel, *open day and groups by appointment*

Boscawen Park (33), Truro

Burncoose (6), nr Redruth, *excluding Suns and Christmas*

Carwinion (36), Mawnan Smith

Cotehele (92), St Dominick, Saltash

Eden Project (63), St Austell, *excluding 24, 25 Dec*

Fox Rosehill (37), Falmouth

Godolphin Estate (10), nr Helston, *for walks*

Gyllyngdune (39), Falmouth

Japanese Garden (67), St Mawgan, *excluding 24 Dec–1 Jan*

Kimberley Park (40), Falmouth

Lanhydrock (69), nr Bodmin

Lanterns (43), Mylor

Long Cross (70), nr Port Isaac

Lost Gardens of Heligan (71), nr St Austell, *excluding 24, 25 Dec*

Lower Bradford Wilderness & Sculpture Garden (72), Blisland, *Suns except Christmas; Apr–Sep also Mons and Thurs*

Menacuddle (74), St Austell

Morrab Gardens (13), Penzance

Mount Edgcumbe (101), Maker

Moyclare (102), Liskeard, *strictly by appointment only*

Paradise Park (14), Hayle

Pengersick Castle (15), Praa Sands, *by appointment*

Penlee Memorial Gardens (16), Penzance

Penrose (17), Hayle, *for walks*

Pinsla Garden (79), Cardinham, nr Bodmin, *daily; Nov–Feb weekends only*

Polgwynne (46), Feock, *by appointment only*

Queen Mary Gardens (47), Falmouth

Roskillys (21), St Keverne

St Just-in-Roseland Churchyard (48), St Just-in-Roseland

Scorrier House (23), Scorrier, *strictly by appointment only*

Tehidy (24), Portreath, nr Redruth

Trebah (51), Mawnan Smith

Tregenna Castle (25), St Ives

Tregullow (26), Redruth, *by request*

Trenance Gardens (86), Newquay

Tresco Abbey Gardens (1), Isles of Scilly

Tresillian House (88), nr Newquay, *groups by appointment only*

Trevarno (27), nr Helston, *excluding 25, 26 Dec*

Victoria Park (58), Truro

## 2 Gardens open in spring and summer

Antony House (89), Torpoint, *Apr–Oct, Tue–Thu; also Suns Jun–Aug*

Antony Woodland (90), Torpoint, *Mar–Oct, excluding Mons and Fris except bank holidays*

Bonython (5), nr Helston, *mid-Apr–mid-Sep, Tue–Thu*

Bosahan (110), Manaccan, *strictly by appointment only*

Bosvigo (34), Truro, *Mar–Sep, Thur–Fri*

Caerhays Castle (61), Gorran, *Mar–Jun*

Carclew (35), Perranarworthal, *Apr–May, Suns, excluding Easter*

Chyverton (112), Zelah, *strictly by appointment only*

Creed House (62), Grampound, *Feb–Oct*

Flambards (8), Helston, *Easter–Oct, see note for exceptions in low season*

Gillhouse (94), nr St Neot, *Apr–Sep, 1st Sun in month, other Suns by appointment*

Glendurgan (38), Mawnan Smith, *mid-Feb–Oct, Tues–Fri and bank holidays except Good Friday*

Godolphin House (10), nr Helston, *Easter–Sep, Tue, Thu, Fri and Sun, enquire for times*

Hidden Valley (65), nr Par, *Mar–Oct*

Ken Caro (98), nr Liskeard, *mid-Apr–*

*Aug, Sun–Thu*

Lamorran House (42), St Mawes, *Apr–Sep, Wed, Fri and 1st Sat in month*

Marsh Villa (73), Par, *Apr–Oct, Sun–Wed*

Mary Newman's Cottage (100), Saltash, *by appointment only*

Oak Lodge (75), nr Bodmin, *Apr–May, Sep–Oct, Fri and Sat, or by appointment*

Old Mill Herbary (76), nr Bodmin, *Apr–Oct, excluding Weds*

Pencarrow (77), nr Bodmin, *Mar–Oct*

Penjerrick (45), Budock Water, *Mar–Sep, Wed, Fri and Sun*

Pine Lodge (78), nr St Austell, *mid-Mar–Oct*

Prideaux Place (81), Padstow, *Easter for 1 week, and May–Oct*

Roseland House (20), Chacewater, *Apr–Sep, Tue and Wed*

St Michael's Mount (22), Marazion, *Apr–May daily; June–Nov, weekends with castle ticket*

Tregrehan (85), nr St Austell, *mid-Mar–mid-Jun, Wed–Sun, excluding Easter; mid-Jun–Aug, Weds only*

Trelissick (53), Feock, *mid-Feb–early Nov*

Trelowarren (27), Mawgan, *Apr–Sep*

Trengwainton (28), Penzance, *mid-Feb–early Nov, excluding Fri and Sat, but open Good Friday*

Trereife (29), Penzance, *from 1st Sun in Aug, daily until 31 Aug*

Trerice (87), nr Newquay, *mid-July–mid-Sep, daily excluding Sats; end Mar–Jun and Oct, daily excluding Tue and Sat*

Trewidden (31), nr Penzance, *mid-Feb–1st week June*

Trewithen (56), nr Truro, *Mar–Sep, Mon–Sat; Apr–May also Suns*

Trist House (57), Veryan, *Apr–Sep, Sun and Tue and by appointment*

## 3 Gardens open only occasionally

*Note that the following gardens are open only at the times stated in the Guide, and cannot be visited at other times. On the larger estates, a charity opening does not imply any public right of way.*

*Gardens asterisked are also open by appointment.*

## February
Trevella (55), nr Truro

## March
Ince Castle (97), nr Saltash
Porthpean (80), nr St Austell
Southfield (107), nr Poundstock
Trevella (55), nr Truro

## April
*Bodwannack (60), nr Bodmin
Higher Truscott (96), nr Launceston
Ince Castle (97), nr Saltash
Ladock House (41), nr Truro
Nansawsan (44), nr Truro
Peterdale (104), nr Torpoint
Porthpean (80), nr St Austell
Tregarthen (52), Veryan
Trevella (55), nr Truro

## May
*Boconnoc (59), nr Lostwithiel
*Bodwannack (60), nr Bodmin
*Fountain Springs (9), Portreath
*Hallowarren (11), Manaccan
Higher Truscott (96), nr Launceston
Ince Castle (97), nr Saltash
Nansawsan (44), nr Truro
Penheale (103), nr Launceston
Peterdale (104), nr Torpoint
Porthpean (80), nr St Austell
Readymoney Cove (82), Fowey
Southfield (107), Poundstock
Springfield Farm (49), nr Truro
Trebartha (108), nr Launceston
*Trenance (109), Launceston
*Trewoofe (32), Lamorna

## June
*Bodwannack (60), nr Bodmin
*Caervallack (7), nr Helston
East Down Barn (93), Menheniot
Higher Truscott (96), nr Launceston
Ince Castle (97), nr Saltash
Landewednack House (12), The Lizard
Long Hay (99), nr Delabole
Penheale (103), nr Launceston
Peterdale (104), nr Torpoint
Readymoney Cove (82), Fowey
Rose Cottage (83), St Breward
*St Martin's Manor (105), Looe
Scawn Mill (106), nr Liskeard
Springfield Farm (49), nr Truro
Talisonny House (50), nr Perranporth
Trebartha (108), nr Launceston
*Trenance (109), Launceston
*Trewoofe (32), Lamorna

## July
Berriow Bridge (91), nr Launceston
Ince Castle (97), nr Saltash
Kingberry (68), Bodmin
Peterdale (104), nr Torpoint
Rose Cottage (83), St Breward
Scawn Mill (106), nr Liskeard
Southfield (107), Poundstock
Springfield Farm (49), nr Truro
Talisonny House (50), nr Perranporth
*Trenance (109), Launceston

## August
*Fountain Springs (9), Portreath
Highcroft Gardens (95), nr Saltash
Tregoose (84), nr Truro
*Trenarth (54), Constantine

## September
Peterdale (104), nr Torpoint
Trebartha (108), nr Launceston

# Index

# Acknowledgements

Photographs are reproduced by kind permission of: Julian Ball, p. 237; Barbara Hepworth Museum/Tate St Ives, pp. 26 (T), 27 (T, BR); John Beckett Photography, p. 177 (B); Mark Brent, p. 104; Ian Browne, p. 105; Burncoose & South Down Nurseries, pp. 30, 31 (T); James Butler, p. 93 (BR); Caerhays Castle, pp. 144–5; Ray & Shirley Clemo, pp. 178, 179; Alison Clough, p. 80; Joyce Cook, p. 119 (T); Cornwall Tourist Board, pp. 138–9; Diana Craig, p. 120; Gillian Dingle, pp. 242 (B), 243 (T); The Eden Project, pp. 148, 149; Flambards Village, pp. 34, 35; Gibsons of Scilly, pp. 14–15, 22 (BR), 23 (T); Valerie Hadley, pp. 54, 55; Elizabeth Henslowe, pp. 228, 229; Jean Hill, pp. 150, 151; Alison Hodge, pp. 11 (B), 24–25, 51 (BL, BR), 66, 67, 86, 87 (T), 117 (BL, BR); James Hodge, pp. 1, 2, 4, 11 (T), 21 (B), 31 (B), 92, 103, 106, 108, 117 (T), 118, 119 (B), 182 (T), 216, 236, 245 (L); G.J. Holborow, p. 102; Sheila Holland, p. 167 (TL, TR); Rob & Stella Hore, pp. 156, 157; Incorporated Arts/Cornwall

Tourist Board, pp. 200–01; Christopher Laughton, p. 62; Tim Le Grice, pp. 76, 77; June Lethbridge, p. 21 (T); Heligan Gardens © David Hastilow, p. 165; Heligan Gardens © Dawn Runnals, p. 164; Anthony Keast, pp. 36, 37; John Mann, p. 217; Mount Edgcumbe/Dick Ogilvie, pp. 226, 227; The National Trust/Andrew Besley, pp. 127 (B), 161 (T), 209 (T); The National Trust/Simon Cook, p. 74; The National Trust/Dan Flunder, pp. 53 (B), 205 (T); The National Trust/David Hastilow, p. 97; The National Trust/Jon Hicks, p. 161 (B), 203 (T), 208 (B), 209 (B); The National Trust/David Judge, pp. 52–3; The National Trust/Tony Kent, pp. 127 (T), 197 (B); The National Trust/Dennis Madge, p. 160; The National Trust/ Charles Mohun, p. 203 (B); The National Trust/Bill Newby, p. 75 (T); The National Trust/ Marcus Way, p. 96; Alison O'Connor, p. 190; K. Olson, pp. 234 (TR), 235; Paradise Park, pp. 11 (M), 46–7; Pencarrow, pp. 176, 177 (T); Michael Perry, pp. 88, 89; Jeremy Peter-Hoblyn, p. 246; Charlotte Petherick, pp. 182 (B), 183; Mrs H.M. Piggott, pp. 82–3; Paddy Powell, pp. 188, 189; Prideaux Place © Rosemary Lauder, pp. 184, 185; Charlie Pridham, pp. 58, 59; B.J. Richards, pp. 214, 215; Matthew Robinson, pp. 32, 33; Jane Rogers, p. 93 (BL); Roskillys, p. 61; Dawn Runnals/Cornwall Tourist Board, pp. 84–5; Joanne Schofield, p. 39; Peter Skerrett, pp. 56, 57 (T); Harriet Stead, pp. 158, 159 (TR); Rob Steerwood, p. 107; Joe Stephens, pp. 40 (B), 41 (T); Judith Stevens, p. 169; Rupert Tenison, p. 63; Trebah Garden Trust, pp. 10, 123; Peregrine Twinkle Treffrey, p. 145 (T); Tregothnan, p. 247 (T); Tresco Estate, pp. 5, 17, 18 (TR), 19; Trevarno Estate, p. 79 (T); Trewidden Estate, p. 81; Trewithen Estate, p. 133; Sir Ferrers Vyvyan, pp. 72, 73; R.D. Whurr, pp. 174, 175; Caroline Williams, pp. 64, 65; Claire Woodbine, pp. 180, 181. All other photographs are by the author.

The map of Boconnoc (p. 8) is taken from *The Parks & Gardens of Cornwall* (Alison Hodge, 1998).

The map inside the back cover is © Collins Bartholomew Ltd 2003 Reproduced by permission of HarperCollins Publishers.